Sales Manager's
Model Letter Desk Book

Sales Manager's
Model Letter Desk Book

Hal Fahner

Morris E. Miller

PARKER PUBLISHING COMPANY, INC.   West Nyack, N.Y.

© 1977 *by*

Parker Publishing Company, Inc.

West Nyack, N.Y.

Twelfth Printing.....April 1987

Library of Congress Cataloging in Publication Data

Fahner, Hal.
    Sales manager's model letter desk book.

    1. Sales letters. 2. Commercial correspondence.
I. Miller, Morris E., joint author. II. Title.
HF5730.F34   658.8'1   76-46994
ISBN 0-13-787663-7

Printed in the United States of America

HAL FAHNER

Hal Fahner has sold products and trained salesmen in such diverse fields as insurance, business services and capital goods. He is presently Sales Training Manager for A.O. Smith Harvestore Products, Inc., in Arlington Heights, Illinois, where he is responsible for sales training and sales management training for a dealership organization of approximately 600 salesmen across the U.S. and Canada.

He also conducts sales management seminars throughout the United States for experienced sales managers as a member of the faculty of the Sales Management Institute sponsored by Sales/Marketing Executives-International, a professional association.

Mr. Fahner is a member of several professional associations and currently Vice President of the Chicago chapter of Sales/Marketing Executives. He is also a member of the William Rainey Harper College Advisory Board for Marketing Mid-Management. He is listed in *Who's Who in Finance and Industry.*

MORRIS E. MILLER

Morris E. Miller is a sales and sales management training consultant with more than 15 years experience in developing sales managers. As the principal in Miller Associates he regularly conducts sales and sales management seminars throughout the country and is nationally recognized as a sales and management authority.

He regularly works with sales managers in organizations of all types—large, small, dealers, distributors, manufacturers, services, wholesalers and retailers.

Prior to his present sales and management consultant relationship, Mr. Miller was sales training director for two multi-million dollar companies and before that was sales manager and salesman for a large manufacturer.

HOW THIS BOOK WILL
HELP YOU WRITE LETTERS THAT
GET ACTION

Right now, do you have a letter that you would just as soon not have to write? Today, how many hours will you spend pondering letters where the words just don't seem to work out right?

How much more productive could you be if you could write a letter so that it conveyed the precise meaning you want it to convey and secured immediate action?

You are now holding in your hands the tool that will help you do exactly that. This book will save you time. It will help you get your message across to your salesmen and customers. It will provide you with the means to light a fire under your salesmen and to get immediate customer action even though you may be hundreds of miles away.

This book contains over 300 tested and successful model letters and alternate phrases. Each one is potential dynamite when you apply it to your letter writing needs. Whenever you are frustrated with that tough-to-write letter, turn to the index, pick out the model letter that fits your situation and dictate away. It's just that simple. Save time? You bet it does, because this book puts at your fingertips the successful letter writing experience of dozens of sales managers from all types of sales organization.

You'll never again waste time and effort trying to compose an effective letter. This compilation of model letters covers every possible situation, occasion or circumstance you will ever be called upon to write a letter for or about. Have you ever spent hours trying to find just the right words to announce a price increase? Chapter 9 will make it easy! Would you like to turn complaints about your product or service into additional sales? The letters in Chapter 11 will help you do just that!

The letters provided in this book have produced results for others; they can also produce results for you. One sales manager submitted a recruiting letter to us and penciled in at the bottom that almost one out of every four salesman prospects he had sent it to responded. Other contributors reported that their letters had made such favorable impressions on customers that the customers had returned the letter with glowing comments penned at the bottom. The letters that have won their way into this book are tested, proven letters. The contributing sales managers who share them with you do so because of their pride in them and the results they achieved.

You will find here the model letters you need to handle almost every conceivable situation: letters for salesmen, letters for customers, letters for collecting past due accounts, letters for sparking the lagging salesmen, letters that turn complaints to compliments, letters that get action from sales contests . . . and hundreds of others.

You will want to keep this book of model letters on your desk within easy reach. Imagine the ease of turning to a model letter, checking off a paragraph or alternate phrase and instructing your secretary to incorporate it in your letter for just the right impact.

A poor letter can cost you sales or a lost account. A careless letter can lose a valuable salesman or cause him to make costly errors. Are your letters causing problems for your salesmen, dissatisfactions among your customers? Take the most recent letter you wrote and compare it with what you find in this book under the appropriate chapter. That difference you see is what sets this book apart and makes it a valuable tool you will want to keep on your desk.

No matter what your situation or your needs, you will find this book valuable. The letters you find here come from some of the world's largest companies, as well as from small and medium-sized companies. Contributions have come from all types of sales organizations—those selling industrial goods, consumer goods and services. They represent manufacturers, distributors, dealers and retailers.

The toughest letter writing situations are covered. Do you have to reduce your best salesman's territory? Run, don't walk, to Chapter 4. Have to say "no" to a good customer who is requesting special terms? The answer is in Chapter 13. One of your servicemen insulted a customer? You'll find help in Chapter 15. You probably haven't tried the approach to a sales contest represented by letter 5-2 in Chapter 5 and it could kick off your most productive contest ever!

You'll also find hundreds of ideas for making your everyday letters more productive. Ever feel salesmen productivity drop off after a sales contest? The ideas in Chapter 1 will keep them producing. Did you ever wish for a smoother way to turn down an unsatisfactory salesman applicant? Chapter 3 has the answer. What about that letter to tell the customer "thanks" without sounding flowery and phony? Try some of the dozens of ideas provided in Chapter 10.

Every letter provided here is ready to use. We have made them even more usable by providing suggestions for alternate wording to meet the variety of needs you might encounter. We have removed the technical information that was contained in the original letters so they could be applied by you more easily and rapidly. The result is a functional, practical and valuable reference tool that will save you time and effort and will improve your letter writing results.

Hal Fahner

Morris E. Miller

ACKNOWLEDGMENTS

Many sales managers shared their most effective letters with us to produce this book. All of the contributors reached their present position from the sales ranks. Their willingness to share ideas with other sales managers is a tribute to their professionalism. Their sales management talents are invaluable and we wish to thank them for their contribution in the name of all the sales managers who will use this book.

Allis-Chalmers Corporation—Charles W. Parker, Corporate Vice-President and Donald F. Thielke, Corporation Public Relations

Blue Cross/Blue Shield of Michigan—Myron T. Abel, Senior Director,Field Sales Department

Bodine Electric—H.M. Fulmer, General Sales Manager

Burgess Vibrocrafters, Inc.—Robert C. Waite, National Sales Manager

Canteen Corporation—Paul G. Duffy, Vice-President-Marketing and Donna J. Click, Coordinator of Merchandising and Communication

Dun & Bradstreet—Paul C. Van Schepen, North Central Zone Manager and Lawrence J. Pace, Product Manager

Durant Digital Instruments—James K. McGinley, President

Fallon Ford, Inc.—Joseph Fallon, President

Fernstrom Moving System—Fred E. Bell, Director, National Account Sales

Hertz Corporation—Marge Larsen, Account Representative

Lawson Products, Inc.—Chester B. Lynn, President

Luxor Corporation—James C. Moran, Sales Manager

Marriott Hotels, Inc.—Steven J. Musatto, National Sales Manager

Midwest Visual Equipment Co., Inc.—Paul Whiteside, Sales Representative

Modern Talking Picture Service—Ed Swanson, Manager Midwest Sales

New York Life Insurance Company—Philip H. Bowers, CLU, General Manager

Fred A. Niles Communications Centers, Inc.—Norman C. Lindquist, Vice-President

Ohio Bell Telephone Company—Jack Criswell, Division Manager and R.L. Schauer, District Community Relations Manager

Ohio Harvestore, Inc.—Bart L. Main, President

Schwinn Bicycle Company—Jack Smith, National Sales Manager

Shalom Memorial Park—Herschel Auerbach, Executive Vice-President

A.O. Smith Corporation—Don Schafer, Regional Sales Manager

United Airlines—Joseph B. Garvey, Manager of Sales and Harry A. Horst, Passenger Sales Manager

Weber Marking Systems, Inc.—James B. Crassweller, Vice-President Marketing

Xerox Learning Systems—Harry W.Blake, District Manager

CONTENTS

Sales Manager's
Model Letter Desk Book

1

LETTERS THAT PROD GOOD SALES PRODUCTION INTO GREAT PRODUCTION

1

LETTERS THAT PROD GOOD SALES PRODUCTION INTO GREAT PRODUCTION

Perhaps nothing is more wasteful than the human potential that is lost as we become satisfied with a minimum performance when much greater achievement is possible. For example, a salesman makes an important sale and then relaxes his effort for the next week as he basks in his accomplishment. Every sales manager can recall such instances. Another salesman reaches a sales goal and becomes complacent and self-satisfied.

Or perhaps you have been aware of the sales lull that often occurs immediately after a successful sales contest. Although part of this drop off may be due to future sales that are telescoped into a contest period, a significant share of the problem lies with the all too human tendency to relax after the extra effort. The salesman may rationalize that all the present customers and prospects are sold for now so continued effort is bound to be fruitless. Or he may feel that after his extra effort during the contest, he deserves a rest. Or he may just feel that now that the contest is over the pressure from the home office will let up for a while, and he can take it a little easier. For whatever reason, the salesman has settled for less than his potential.

Your written communication with your salesmen can be a valuable tool for spurring success into even greater success. The letters we have included in this section have been proven useful for this purpose. Most of them are similar in that they contain two essential elements:

1. A reward—The behaviorial scientists have confirmed through research that we all work to satisfy certain needs. The salesman will be motivated to put forth extra effort if his job offers him the possibility for satisfying any of these needs.

    a) The salesman will put forth extra effort for recognition—a pat on the back. It is not just recognition from the boss he seeks, but also from other salesmen, from his wife, from others in the community. Providing the recognition he seeks will spur the salesman to greater production.

    b) The salesman will put forth extra effort for a sense of accomplishment—a feeling that he is providing some worthwhile value to the company, to other employees, to the community, to his family. Although money the salesman receives provides a portion of this sense of accomplishment, (for what is money but a measure of his value) the sales manager can supplement and emphasize the sense of accomplishment the job provides.

    c) The salesman will put forth extra effort for a sense of participation in the decisions which affect him. He wants to feel that the boss and the company value his suggestions. He wants to have some influence on the decisions that affect him. The sales manager who seeks his salesman's contributions can often motivate him to ever greater performance.

    d) Salesmen will put forth extra effort for the opportunity for growth and advancement. Younger salesmen need to become professional in their sales skills. Others are seeking an opportunity to prepare for management positions.

2. A challenge—This is the "carrot" that is held out suggesting even greater rewards for additional effort. It encourages the salesman to carry on to greater accomplishment. Where the reward focuses on past performance, the challenge directs attention to future opportunity.

1. CONGRATULATIONS ON AN OUTSTANDING SALE

When a salesman makes that extraordinary sale, it's an experience to be shared. Even though he receives a handsome commission for his effort, he seeks a reward that, to him, may be even more important—recognition. Provide recognition and you set the stage for further effort; ignore it and it could be the last such sale he makes.

Notice that the model letter is specific about what the salesman has accomplished. Not only does this help the salesman to recognize exactly what it is that you are complimenting him on, it lets him know you care enough to dig out the details.

Timing, as in all motivational letters, is important. Let the salesman know you are aware of his accomplishment as soon as you learn about it. Also valuable: let others important to the salesman know what he has been able to accomplish—then tell him that you have spread the word.

Model Letter 1-1

Dear _____

It doesn't often happen and when it does it's something to **(a)** shout about!

I'm referring to your recent sale to Central Wholesale Hardware. Not only is this dealer one of the largest in the Division, it's one we have been trying unsuccessfully to land for a long time. And the fact that you accomplished this feat single handedly from initial proposal to close adds immeasurably to your credit.

So shout is what I've been doing. The Vice President of Sales **(b)** has heard all about what you have been able to do and so has the Product Manager.

Now's the time to review what you did to bring off this achievement so you can regularly apply the techniques to some of your other important prospects. Perhaps you would like to take a few minutes at next month's sales meeting to tell everyone how you were able to bring it off.

Sincerely,

P.S.   I've placed a copy of this letter in your personnel jacket. It may be of value for future considerations.

Alternate Wording:

(a)   I just got word on your terrific achievement.

(a)   I was just looking over your sales call report and was overjoyed to notice an outstanding accomplishment.

(b)   I'm like the proud dad that has to brag about his son's accomplishments. And am I bragging. V.P. Bill Johnson was the first to hear. He would like to have you tell him about it personally the first time you are in the office. Also, your outstanding accomplishment will be in next week's sales newsletter.

2.   CONGRATULATIONS ON WINNING A SALES CONTEST

A sales contest by its very nature provides winners with desired recognition. However, you can get considerably more mileage by careful wording of your letter of congratulation. This model letter helps you realize extra benefits from a contest not only by patting the salesman on the back but by pointing him toward even greater achievements to come.

Notice the conciseness of this letter making it suitable for framing. It's difficult to frame a two page letter.

Model Letter 1-2

Dear _____

Congratulations on winning first place in the Region 76 "Plus 10" drive. Signing fifteen new accounts during the sixty day contest is a remarkable achievement.

I'm sure you worked both smarter and harder in the past sixty days. And I'm sure the rewards you will enjoy as a result go far beyond the winning of the contest. To highlight only one—the feeling of a job well done must be in your mind. And it deserves to be. **(a)**

Your wife, Barbara, must be proud of your accomplishment and her support must have been most important to you as you made those extra calls.

When you and Barbara return from your award trip, we **(b)** should discuss the sales techniques you found that most helped you win the contest. We have a great opportunity this year and the thought you invested during this contest can continue to pay you big dividends in increased sales and commissions.

Sincerely,

Alternate Wording:

(a) Your wife, Barbara, must be proud of your accomplishment and her support must have been most important to you as you made those extra calls. I have taken the opportunity to send her a note explaining what you have been able to accomplish during this contest.

(a) I have taken the liberty to provide a press release to your local newspaper apprising them of your achievement.

(b) Enclosed is your first place award check for $_____. You probably have already become aware that this extra money can be yours each and every month by continuing with the effort and techniques you have used during the contest. Your commissions for the new business you sold during the contest period nearly equals the award check.

Is it a goal worth shooting for?

3. FOR THE SALESMAN'S PART IN HELPING THE SALES OFFICE WIN A SALES CONTEST

Most salesmen respond positively when asked to contribute to a team effort. This is a need that springs from their desire for participation. The key to successful motivation through team effort is adequate and prompt follow-up recognition. Here is a letter that provides such recognition and, in addition, encourages the salesman to even greater achievements.

Model Letter 1-3

Dear _____

We're Number 1. And the $126,543 in business you wrote during the contest period made the difference. As you know, Los Angeles was ahead of us during most of the contest. Only in the last week were we able to pull $23,000 ahead of them. If it were not for your extra effort (or for that matter the extra effort of any other member of this great sales team) it would have been a different story.

But we can't let down now. Los Angeles will be gunning for **(a)** us. Let's not let them throw in our face that we won the contest, but only at the expense of future sales. *Keep the pressure on.*

From me and all the other salesmen on the team, thanks for a job well done.

Sincerely,

Alternate Wording:

(a) As you may know, no division has been successful in keeping a position of number one for two consecutive quarters. I believe we're in a position to pull it off. Keep up the extra effort and we will be the shining star division of the company.

(a) As you may know, no division has been successful in keeping the number one position for two consecutive quarters, I believe we're in a position to pull it off. How would it feel to be a member of a team to accomplish something that's never been done before?

Here is a letter written by a sales manager whose salesmen didn't quite win the contest, but deserved a pat on the back anyway.

Model Letter 1-4

Dear _____

Well, as it turns out we're number two. But that only means we will have to try harder. The Midwest Division beat us by

just $62,000. That represents only about two sales from each
of you.   (a)

But let me personally thank you for the extra effort that was
so visible from you during this contest period. Your sales are
up over $9,000 and it's easy to see from your sales call reports
just what has led to the sales increase—plenty of extra hard
work and extra hours.

I personally believe we still deserve to be number one . As a
matter of fact I am so sure of it that I suggested to Midwest
that we would beat them in total sales during the coming
quarter. They're willing to take us on. An extra three sales
per week would make the difference. How about it? Shall I
tell them they have a bet?

Sincerely,

Alternate Wording:
(a)   The sales bet we had with the Midwest Division cost us a lit-
        tle money, but a lot of pride. It's not easy to take a back seat
        to Midwest.

4. FOR SUGGESTIONS USED BY THE SALES OFFICE

Suggestions and recommendations from the sales force are not
only an important source of new ideas for improving the efficiency and
sales of the organization, they are a means, if handled properly, for
salesman motivation. When the sales manager solicits and accepts the
ideas of his salesmen, it's an indication he values their opinions. It tells
the salesman he is needed and important and that he makes an important contribution to the organization. The following letter taps this
idea source and motivates the sales force to greater productivity.

Model Letter 1-5

Dear _____

We all know that our new HY-POX industrial glove has
some very desirable qualities for use by the chemical industry. We also know it takes more than telling our
customers about the tremendous advantages we have to offer.

Here's an opportunity to make an "above-the-call-of-duty" contribution to the company and your sales teammates. If you have found ways to demonstrate the unique qualities of the HY-POX line, let us know about it.

To be more specific, we need ways to demonstrate:
- The toughness of the HY-POX line;
- The acid resistant quality of the line;
- The dexterity quality of the line;
- The wearing comfort of the line.

Send your ideas to me. I'll make sure they are circulated to **(a)** the entire sales force. Besides providing a valuable service to thhe others in the organization, you will have the satisfaction of seeing your ideas grow and produce results.

Sincerely,

Alternate Wording;

(a) Dick Spencer has recently sent to me an excellent idea for demonstrating HY-POX's acid resistant quality. I will be forwarding the idea to you in a few days. If you have ideas, send them along. I'll make sure they are distributed to all salesmen.

(a) Just to make it interesting, here is a little contest. When all the ideas are published, we will ask each salesman to vote on the most valuable demonstration idea. The salesmen who submit the three ideas judged most valuable by the sales force will each win $50.

Here is a letter that thanks the salesman for his contribution and informs him that his idea will be used by the organization. Note the specific reference to the suggestion the salesman made.

Model Letter 1-6

Dear _____

We are modifying the sales call report as you suggested.

The addition of a results column and the use of a third copy for comparing results with plans will undoubtedly improve the planning and call efficiency of many salesmen. New forms are being printed and will be sent to all salesmen next month.

Thanks for your idea not only from me but from the other **(a)** salesmen as well. Keep the ideas coming in. I value them as an "on the firing line" practical source.

Alternate Wording:

(a) As a special token of the sales department's appreciation for your idea, would you and Sue please accept dinner some evening at the restaurant of your choice. Just put the bill on your expense account.

Keep the new ideas coming in. It's only through ideas such as yours that this company can keep ahead of competition.

The sales manager encounters another communication problem when the salesman provides a suggestion that cannot be utilized by the organization. He must indicate to the salesman that his idea is unacceptable, but must do it in such a way that he encourages future contributions. Here is such a model letter. Note the letter's positive tone.

Model Letter 1-7

Dear _____

Thanks for your suggestion concerning modification of our 260 Model Air Conditioner. It's through recommendations such as yours that we can be sure our air conditioner line is kept current with the needs of our customers. It's obvious that you have given considerable thought to your recommendation.

Your suggestion would probably have been accepted if it had **(a)** meshed with the long range marketing plans for the product. The intention is to keep this line as a low cost conditioner which appeals to a mass market. Your recommendation, although significant, would increase the cost of the conditioner beyond the competitive level.

The spirit with which you made your recommendation is commendable. Engineering and marketing need your suggestions. Keep them coming. Next time it may just be the most important contribution the company receives all year.

Sincerely,

Alternate Wording:

(a) Engineering has considered your suggestion and feels that, although the benefits would be worthwhile, the technical complexity of the modification would subject the conditioner to frequent and costly repairs. For this reason they feel your suggestion must await the time when simpler methods of application are developed.

5. ENCOURAGING SUPPORT FROM A SPOUSE

An important source of back-up support is obtained from the salesman's wife. If she understands and supports the salesman's efforts, she will assist him to greater effort and success. If she fails to understand and accept his being away from home overnight, his working extra hours, or resists accompanying him when he entertains clients, she can quickly destroy your most intent motivational efforts. Many sales managers continually work to keep the wife informed and to show appreciation for her support. This letter fits this category.

Model Letter 1-8

Dear _____

I can't tell you how much it meant to us and to all the men who attended the National Sales Conference last week to have Dave assist as one of the instructors in our seminar programs.

As you already know, Dave has a tremendous amount of talent and experience and his willingness to share his knowledge with the newer men as well as those who have been with the company for some time, was truly appreciated by everyone present.

I know it was an imposition on you and on Dave to ask him to come in early because it meant he would be away from home a little longer than would normally be the case,—and, of course, we realize that some time was lost from his territory. However, I'm sure you will find that the results will be a gain in the productiveness of the men he taught, but, also, you will find that he, too, has learned a great deal from the experience. It is true that the teacher always learns just about as much from his students as they do from him.

Thanks again for your understanding and your kind co-operation.

Sincerely,

6. FOR REACHING A GOAL

Sales and personal goals can be a highly motivating force—but only if the sales manager makes reaching them important. This letter was written to recognize the outstanding efforts of the salesman to reach a goal and to encourage him to continue striving to meet new goals.

Model Letter 1-9

Dear _____

When you and I sat down to work out your goal plan for the year, I believe we agreed that yours was an ambitious goal that would require a great amount of extra effort and smart selling. I also said that I believed you had what it would take to meet the goal.

It's nice to be proved correct. Congratulations on meeting your sales goals right down the line. What you have been able to accomplish called for innovative selling, persistence and a willingness to sacrifice.

Enclosed is your bonus check that you have earned as a **(a)** result of meeting your goals.

Today's accomplishments, as great as they are, become **(b)** tomorrow's base from which to work. I know from my previous experience with you that you will want to move on from here to greater ccomplishments. Let's plan on meeting next Monday morning to establish your next year's goals.

Sincerely,

Alternate Wording:

(a) Enclosed is your bonus check that you have earned as a result of meeting your goals. In addition, Mr. Harris has requested that we have a small get-together dinner for all the salesmen and their wives who, such as you, have been so successful in the past year. I will be letting you know shortly about the details of that dinner.

(b) Now, since this is an "I love you greatly, but what have you done for me lately" organization, I know you will want to be thinking what you intend to accomplish during the coming year. Now's the time to take a fresh assessment of your assets and your needs to determine what you can reasonably expect to achieve in the coming plan period. I'll be setting a date with you during the next week.

2

MODEL LETTERS THAT SPUR SALESMEN TO ACT ON YOUR SUGGESTIONS

2

MODEL LETTERS THAT SPUR
SALESMEN TO ACT ON YOUR
SUGGESTIONS

A new idea is too frequently like the proverbial seed that falls on barren ground—it fails to take root and grow. One of the sales manager's most frustrating experiences is to give instructions or suggestions to his salesmen to see them only minimally carried out or ignored.

Although the sales manager can order that his ideas be put into action, he runs the risk that unless the salesman is convinced of the wisdom of the idea, he will obey only to the extent necessary to "get the sales manager off his back." The logic and wisdom of an idea must be sold to the salesman before he will take the suggestion and run with it. In addition, he must see what's in it for him—how he stands to benefit from the extra effort you are asking him to exert.

Conveying ideas to the sales force that is geographically dispersed is of additional difficulty. If the communication is important enough, the salesman or the entire force can be brought to the home office. If the subject is not of an urgent nature, discussion might be postponed until the manager and salesman are next together. There remain, however, considerable occasions when the sales manager must convey ideas to a salesman where personal "eye-to-eye" communication is not practical.

There remains the telephone or the letter. The telephone is a valuable method for selling your ideas because of its immediacy and because of the personal and informal nature it provides to communication. However, the risk is ever present that the more subtle aspects of the sales manager's suggestion will be lost through the verbal nature of the telephone. Research has taught us that when we rely on the ear alone as a message receiver, no more than 30% of the communication is likely to be retained. When the eye can be included as a receiver, the retention can be expected to jump to as much as 80% or more. The message is clear—the letter has a definite place in getting your ideas across to the salesman, even in this age of electronic communication.

The telephone and the letter can often be used in combination to derive a type of synergistic effect providing combined benefits that are greater than the sum of both. The telephone can be used to provide an initial understanding of the idea. A letter can provide written follow-up to put the idea in perspective and to provide a written summary of key points as a reminder to the salesman. Conversely, a letter can be used to introduce the idea with a telephone follow-up to check understanding. Either method will often result in greater understanding than one used alone.

Getting your ideas and suggestions put into action by means of a letter is not different from the personal sales job you do when convincing a salesman in person to use an idea. The following model letters generally rely on a four step approach to convince the reader to take action on the manager's idea.

1. The writer secures the reader's interest in what he wants to suggest. To do this, he appeals to the selfish interest of the reader.
2. He discusses the problem which has required that the letter be written.
3. He develops a solution to the problem with a description of personal benefits that will accrue to the salesman.
4. He asks for a definite action by the salesman.

1. INFORMING SALESMAN ABOUT NEW MARKET OR PRODUCT APPLICATION

A new market or application for your product offers new sales and profit opportunities. When such an opportunity is recognized, several or all of your salesmen will likely be involved. Unless the new market or product application involves sophisticated or difficult to explain concepts, a letter will probably be the most efficient method for informing your sales force.

Model Letter 2-1

Dear _____

What if within your territory you were able to find more than **(a)** $720,000 per year from a single new market? What would it take to convince you to go after it?

- Proof that you could tap it?
- A tested method for selling it?
- The sales tools for making a meaningful presentation?

As a company, we have done little to tap the car dealer market. In your territory alone there are over 35 new automobile dealers. Only one of these do we sell. According to our marketing research data, the average automobile dealership purchases over $20,000 in lubricants and oil yearly. By selling four of these dealers in the coming twelve months, you would generate an extra $80,000 in sales.

Can it be done? No question about it. During a test period, we chose four sales territories to develop a market approach. Over a four month trial period, the salesmen were able to generate over $350,000 in added sales (projected on a yearly basis) through this lucrative market.

How did they do it? With this simple organized plan.

1. Identify your market. Who are the car dealers in your territory? To simplify your job, I am enclosing a list of automobile dealers in your territory. Note that the sales volume of each is indicated. I would suggest that you concentrate your efforts on the largest.

2. Develop an approach for presenting our car dealer program. The key elements are identified in the flip chart presentation which has been developed for the campaign. You might also want to talk with the management of the car dealer which we now service to determine the benefits of our program from his point of view.

3. Make an appointment for your interview. We have found that the best interest-getter for securing an interview is to suggest that we are happy to use our credit card program as a means for extending ready credit to the dealer's customers at no cost to the dealership. During our test program, 62% of those called for an appointment responded favorably to this lead. Be sure to interview the right man. In most dealerships this will be the owner or general manager.

4. Make your presentation. See the description below of supporting sales tools which are provided.

5. Make a formal proposal. We will help here. Just provide us with name, address, estimated volume, key interest areas and what it will take to get the account. We will send a formal proposal to the individual you suggest with a copy to you.

6. Follow-up to get action. Make a follow-up call within ten working days.

Here's what we are supplying to make this job easy and successful for you: (All materials are being mailed this week)

- A flip chart presentation to assist you identify the main features of our car dealer program and the benefits provided.
- A detailed brochure describing our credit card program for car dealers.
- A product brochure of lubricants for car dealer applications.
- Car dealer testimonials that you can include in your presentation.

Immediately, send me your goal for: **(b)**

1. How many car dealers you expect to sell each quarter of the next 12 months;

2. How many formal presentations you expect to make to car dealer prospects for each quarter of the next 12 months;

3. How many car dealer prospects you expect to call for an appointment for each quarter of the next 12 months.

I will be expecting your goal estimates by May 15.

Sincerely,

Alternate Wording:

(a) Would you be interested in earning an additional $1200 in bonus this coming year? Our market test department has proved it can be done in a sales territory very similar to your own. How was it done?

(b) Please call me on Wednesday, May 15, so we can discuss this plan. Be prepared to ask any questions that will help your understanding and be prepared to tell me how you plan to implement the program.

2. INFORMING THE SALESMAN ABOUT ANOTHER'S SUCCESSFUL METHODS

How do you get a salesman to accept the successful techniques that are used by another salesman? The difficulty in getting such new ideas accepted and used lies with the defense mechanism in the salesman's mind that reacts when he is asked to take on the ideas of a peer. Here's a letter that does the job.

Model Letter 2-2

Dear _____

Time is money. It's been said so often that it's almost trite. (a) Yet just last week a friend of yours proved how true that idea really is.

Brian Watts has made a practice of checking with the prospect's banker sometime after making his first call and before making a presentation. Brian admits it takes some time to accomplish this. He has had to work with the bankers in his territory to get them to cooperate. But after that it takes only a telephone call to determine if the prospect has the financial capacity to buy.

Brian reports that just last week he made a check with a banker on a prospect only to discover the prospect is in deep financial trouble. Had he failed to make his check, it would have cost him an estimated ten to twelve hours of sales time only to learn the prospect couldn't be sold. Now he's more sold than ever on the wisdom of checking first with the banker.

There's another advantage to qualifying the prospect by first checking with the banker—You can often develop some added helpful information about the prospect that will assist you in selling him.

Can you line up the cooperation of just two bankers in your **(b)** territory as a starter? Some time invested in this direction now can mean many more profitable hours in actual selling time later.

Would you indicate your reaction by return mail?

Sincerely,

Alternate Wording:

(a) Think back over your prospect list for the past month. How many prospects have you thought you had sold only to find they couldn't finance their purchase?

      Brian Watts did just that a few months ago and found that he was losing considerable time for profitable selling by trying to sell the prospect who didn't have the financial capacity to buy. As a result he has made a practice of checking with the prospect's banker sometime after making his first call and before making . . .

(b) I would like to have your ideas on how you would put a program like this into operation in your own area. Think it through and let me have the results sometime in the next week.

3. SUGGESTING EMPHASIS ON A PARTICULAR PRODUCT

There are times when every sales manager must direct the efforts of his sales force toward a particular product. Perhaps his salesmen are neglecting a high profit line. Or inventories may be out of line requiring concentrated sales effort to recover working capital. These are situations for which a sales force letter is particularly well suited.

Model Letter 2-3

Dear _____

Help! Your special effort is needed. The company is being (a) choked with oversized inventories in our 360 and 660 models. Sluggish sales in these lines during the past six months have swollen our inventory.

To assist you in moving the excess fast, you are authorized to offer 22% off normal dealer price until June 30. All orders must be shipped by the June 30th date to qualify.

Here's where you personally benefit. For every unit you sell in either the 360 or 660 line between now and June 30, you will earn an additional $3.00 spiff.

Now's your chance to earn several hundred dollars in extra commission. Here's how:

1. Begin today to check dealer stock for adequate inventory.
2. Get POP displays out front where they sell.
3. Sell for inventory. Dealers can make big profit by stocking ahead.
4. Talk the 360 and 660 line to everyone you call on.

I will be checking weekly with you on this important sales effort. We must reduce inventory Now.

Sincerely,

Alternate Wording:

(a) Looking for some extra cash? Here's a fast way to get it and at the same time be of service to your dealers.

Sluggish sales in our 360 and 660 models have pushed up inventorie. To work them off we are authorized to offer a 22% off dealer list discount until June 30.

Here is a letter that was written to place special emphasis on a product where high profit potential was being missed.

Model Letter 2-4

Dear _____

Profit is the name of the game. Each and every one of us **(a)** must put maximum emphasis where the greatest profit for the company is to be made. And of course you are aware that the Golden Imperial line is where the profit is.

In your own territory, Golden Imperial accounts for 30% of your sales and over 45% of the gross profit generated. An extra 10% in sales would increase profit by 21%.

Such an increase in the Golden Imperial line should be readily available to you. Your premium line sales are 6% lower than the national average, although I am sure you will agree that your territory has more than an average number of quality stores.

I believe you can pull off a 10% increase in the Golden **(b)** Imperial line. Such a success would put you well ahead of the pack and would put you in a good position to win the salesman of the year award in December.

Might I suggest that you make this your personal goal. Send back to me in the next week a plan of action that will enable you to achieve this important goal. Then perhaps we can get together by telephone to discuss your approach and arrive at a final plan. I'll look forward to hearing from you.

Sincerely,

Alternate Wording:

(a) Is "profit" a dirty word? Not in this company. That's what we're in business for. And one way to increase company profits is to increase the sales of our Golden Imperial line.

(b) A 21% profit increase for your territory would put you up among the top two or three most profitable territories in the Division. And that would make a nice feather for your cap. After all, territory profitability is one of the factors considered in management placement considerations.

4. SUGGESTING TARGET ACCOUNTS

If (to adapt an old saw) your salesman can't see the tree for the forest, you may need this type of letter to call his attention to an important prospect opportunity.

Model Letter 2-5

Dear _____

The climate may be just about right for you to make a call on:

> Acme Tool and Grinding
> 132 East Front Street
> Middletown, _____
> Steel Purchasing contact: John Garcia

As you may be aware, this prospect is a customer of Bryson, Inc. I have an indication they are having some trouble getting satisfactory delivery on some of their tool steel. So now might be a perfect time to make an appointment. I will be watching your call reports for the results.

Sincerely,

5. ENCOURAGING A SALESMAN TO USE A COACHING SUGGESTION

Letters can be a valuable aid in getting the salesman to put into action suggestions you have made during personal coaching sessions. During the hustle-bustle of the coaching activity, suggestions may be lost and concepts may become obscure. A follow-up letter draws attention to a particular discussion area and puts in writing the main points discussed. Here is such a letter.

Model Letter 2-6

Dear _____

Tuesday and Wednesday were interesting and profitable days. Not only were some very important sales made, you gave me some excellent ideas to pass on to the other salesmen. I hope you got some new ideas as well.

Wednesday afternoon we talked about the need to develop a clear-cut list of benefits your prospect could expect to receive as a result of buying your product. This point is so important that it would bear repeating here. The prospect is interested in the features of your product only to the extent that they will help him to satisfy some need. Don't assume he will readily see the connection between the feature and the need he wishes to satisfy. It's a dangerous assumption, for it can cost you a sale. Be careful to clearly describe each benefit especially as you feel it will be important to the prospect.

The result of this close tailoring of benefits to prospect needs of course will be greater sales. I'm sure that is of great importance to you as you develop your territory.

Work on this area for the next week and when we get (a) together again on the 18th, we'll discuss how you have been progressing. I know you will find that your prospect's interest and desire will sharpen considerably.

Thanks again for a very worthwhile two days last week.

Sincerely,

Alternate Wording:

(a)   Just to sharpen your skill in translating features to customer benefits, when you are planning each sales call for the coming week, take each feature of the product you intend to discuss and write out the benefits you feel will be important to the prospect. Hold on to your list and we will discuss it when we are together on the 18th.

3

EFFECTIVE LETTERS TO ATTRACT TOP SALES PRODUCERS TO YOUR ORGANIZATION

3

EFFECTIVE LETTERS TO ATTRACT TOP SALES PRODUCERS TO YOUR ORGANIZATION

For most sales managers, recruiting new salesmen is a task largely involving written communication. An ad must be placed in various newspapers. An agency must be contacted. Each reply must be acknowledged whether the respondent seems to be qualified or not. Additional information may be required above what the respondent supplied with his initial response. Requests for interviews must be extended. Offers of employment must be made. Your salesmen candidates will be influenced largely by the letters you write. Stuffy, formal letters will convey to them a similar sales organization. Lively and well conceived letters will attract the top producers. When you must turn away the unqualified applicant, you must do it in such a way that his good will is preserved. While he may not meet your requirements as a salesman, he may make a good customer, or he may know those who are.

1. SOLICITING SALESMAN CANDIDATES LEADS

The really outstanding salesman is worth searching for. That means effort beyond running an ad in the newspaper. Some companies constantly communicate with other companies, employees, customers, etc. searching for prospective salesmen. The following letter is used periodically even though no openings exist at that moment. Experience has taught this company that openings occur frequently enough to be searching constantly for qualified people.

Model Letter 3-1

Dear _____

In three minutes you can do someone a big favor and it won't cost you a dime!

There very well may be mature people you know who should be in or taking a look at the life insurance industry. _____Life Insurance Company has positions open in sales and management for both men and women.

With our ever expanding base of insurance programs and **(a)** marketing depth, unique opportunities are present for persons with successful experience or interest in insurance or other sales fields.

Just write the names of people you think might like to receive **(b)** a free copy of an informative pamphlet entitled "Selecting Your Life Work."

Do it now, please. Your friends will appreciate it and so will I.

Thanks.

Sincerely,

Alternate Wording:

(a) We have a unique opportunity for the right man. The individual we seek, has at least three years of successful sales experience in industrial equipment. He is a college graduate, is currently employed and is ambitiously watching for a better opportunity.

(b) If such an individual comes to mind, just jot his name and address or telephone number at the bottom of this letter and return it to me in the enclosed self-addressed envelope.

Letter indicating interest in a
recommended salesman who has not applied
for employment

Occasionally, you hear about that extraordinary salesman already employed who is worth going after. Perrhaps its the result of the letter that is suggested above. Or perhaps a customer or acquaintance has volunteered a prospect. This letter is used by a company to lead off in an initial approach to the prospective salesman candidate.

Model Letter 3-2

Dear _____

Your name has been referred to us most favorably. We have **(a)** no way of knowing whether this will be of interest to you or if you are perfectly satisfied in your present situation.

We have an opening in sales which can be very lucrative for the right person. If you would like to explore your possibilities in this growth industry please call me at _____. If I am not in, leave your phone number with my secretary along with the most convenient time to reach you. **(b)**

Sincerely,

Alternate Wording:

(a) Your name has been referred to us most favorably by _____. (Better get permission of the referral source to use his name—but this will strengthen your approach.)

(b) We have a sales opening that may offer you new opportunity for growth, increased earnings and work satisfaction.

A letter in response to a blind inquiry

Most sales offices frequently receive resumes and inquiries initiated by individuals who have no direct knowledge of actual sales openings. The following letter can be used where there are no openings at that time or where the individual appears to lack the necessary qualifications for openings that exist.

Model Letter 3-3

Dear _____

Thank you for your recent letter and information concerning your background and experience.

We do not have a position available presently that would meet your requirements or experience.

If we have an opening in the next few months and it appears your qualifications match our requirements, I will contact you.

Thank you for thinking of our company in your search for new opportunity.

Sincerely,

Letter indicating interest and acknowledging receipt of resume

When you are in the midst of an all out recruiting campaign to fill one or more sales positions, you will sometimes receive many responses in a short period of time. It may be physically impossible to personally contact each respondent immediately. But you don't want to lose the interest of any of the respondents—you don't know which one of them might be potentially your top producer next year. You should respond to all applicants immediately indicating an interest in them and providing information to maintain their interest in your openings while you organize all of the information you have received and prepare for interviews.

Model Letter 3-4

Dear _____

Thank you for your resume. It looks as if you have some important qualifications and experience that might fit the requirements for the position we have open.

I have attached a brochure describing our company and (a)
products. I hope that material will give you additional insight
into the background and nature of our business.

I will be in Chicago next week for interviews and look
forward to meeting with you. I will phone you later this week
to set up an appointment.

Sincerely,

Alternate Wording:

(a) I have attached a copy of our annual report which describes
our company and products.

Model Letter 3-5

Dear _____

Thank you for your response to our advertisement. Your
reply is one of many we are processing to determine whom
we will ask to interview with us. We want you to know we are
interested in you on the basis of the resume you sent.

Sorry for the delay, but we will be in contact with you in a
few days.

Sincerely,

**Requesting additional information from
a sales candidate**

Sometimes you will receive a response from a prospective
salesman which does not provide as much initial information as you
would like. It may be in the best interest of both the candidate and the
sales manager to get that basic background information before investing the time and expense of telephone and/or face to face interviews.

Model Letter 3-6

Dear _____

Thank you for your interest in our sales position opening.
As our next step, we request that you complete the enclosed

application and return it to us at your earliest convenience. Please complete the application in its entirety. Information concerning our company is attached for your perusal.

After we have had an opportunity to review your application we will contact you.

Thank you for your interest in our organization. We look forward to hearing from you in the very near future.

Sincerely,

Indicating the desire for an interview with a sales candidate

When you have reviewed the initial background information the candidate has provided and have decided it looks like there is a possibility of a match, you will want to arrange an interview. This letter explains what will be involved in the interview and helps the salesman to be prepared for the interview.

Model Letter 3-7

Dear _____

Thank you for responding to our ad in the *Tribune*. Your **(a)** resume in particular is of interest to me. I would like to discuss your experience in our industry further with you to see if this experience and your abilities could be successfully applied to our sales position.

I would like to meet with you at my office either next Wednesday or Thursday at 4:00 p.m. and we should be finished by 5:30 p.m. Please phone my secretary at _____ to confirm one of these dates or an alternate time if neither of these is possible for you.

I look forward to meeting with you.

Sincerely,

Alternate Wording:

(a) Your resume is interesting. We would like to discuss with you in more detail how your qualifications might match the needs of our job opening.

**Declining employment to a prospective
salesman without an interview**

Some applicants for employment will be obviously unqualified. In screening application forms and resumes, you will find some who will simply not meet company standards of education, experience or other requirement. Respond promptly to all applicants even though they fail to meet your minimum requirements. Permitting them to wonder what happened to their application is bad public relations. Your letter to these applicants should tell them definitely that they do not qualify at present, but in a way that will not alienate or insult them. After all, they may gain the necessary qualifications and reapply in the future. And they may be potential buyers of your products or services.

Model Letter 3-8

Dear _____

Recently you expressed interest in pursuing a sales career with our company by sending your resume. During the past week I have reviewed your and many other applicants' resumes. While your work experience and education are impressive, I have concluded that they do not specifically meet our desired criteria.   **(a)**

Your resume will be kept on file, for we are a dynamic, grow- **(b)**
ing company and consequently anticipate many future employment needs. When some of these opportunities become available, your resume will again be considered.

Thank you for your interest in our company.

Sincerely,

Alternate Wording:

(a) Your work experience and education are impressive but do not exactly match the requirements of our present opening.

(b) Your resume will be kept on file for the next six months. We will continue to consider you for similar job openings as they occur during that time. If you should desire to be considered after the six month period, you should resubmit an updated resume at that time.

Declining employment to a prospective
salesman after an interview

Intensive recruiting efforts should develop more salesman prospects than you have openings to fill. These additional prospects can provide a pool that may be tapped as future openings occur. The letter you send to the refused applicant must be carefully worded so that you inform him that he will not get the job, but preserves his good will so he may be expected to respond favorably should another opening occur.

Model Letter 3-9

Dear _____

I enjoyed meeting with you last week.

We received over one hundred applications and you should be pleased to know that you were one of our final candidates. Unfortunately, we had only one opening and only one man could get the job.   (a)

I want to thank you sincerely for the time and effort you invested in exploring the possibilities with our company. I am going to keep your resume in the front of my file and hope that the growth of our company will provide another opportunity for us to work together.

I am sure that your talent and ambition will lead you to an interesting, challenging, and rewarding future.

Thanks again for your interest in our company.

Sincerely,

Alternate Wording:

(a) I want to emphasize that the man we hired had the advantage of a background which fit our opening perfectly. I only wish we had another position to offer you.

2. OFFERING EMPLOYMENT TO A SALESMAN CANDIDATE

When you ultimately determine the best candidate for your job opening, your letter of tender should be so structured that it reminds him of the advantages of joining your organization and encourages him to make a positive decision.

Model Letter 3-10

Dear _____

I know you will be pleased to learn that in our estimation your experience, background and knowledge puts you in a position to be highly successful in the job opportunity we discussed recently. We invite you to join our company as sales representative.

As we discussed, when you have accepted this offer you will have the opportunity to complete our unique training program in Chicago. After nine weeks, you will be assigned to a territory yet to be determined.

As we discussed your salary while in training will be $_____. When you are assigned, your salary will be $_____ and you will earn a commission of _____.

You have impressed us with your talent and successful experience. I hope you will decide to accept this offer which will be held open until July 31. When you decide to accept, call me collect and we will work out the details.

Congratulations, and I will look forward to your telephone call.

Sincerely,

3. CLOSING CORRESPONDENCE WITH A SALESMAN WHO HAS DECLINED YOUR FIRM OFFER OF EMPLOYMENT

Unfortunately every employment offer you tender will not necessarily result in acceptance. In such situations you owe one final letter to the salesman candidate who has refused your offer. Your letter should be structured in such a manner that you not only keep the door open for future employment possibilities but maintain positive public relations.

Model Letter 3-11

Dear _____

We want to thank you sincerely for your interest in our sales position. We respect your decision to remain with your present organization and wish you success in pursuing your career goals.

As we told you, we believe your experience and abilities would have suited you for a successful career with our growing sales organization.

If circumstances should change in the future, we would be interested in again discussing with you the employment opportunities in our company.

Sincerely,

4. WELCOMING THE NEW EMPLOYEE TO THE ORGANIZATION

When he accepts employment, there is one last letter to write. This model letter is designed to welcome the new employee to your organization and to make him feel at home.

Model Letter 3-12

Dear _____

We want you to know it's a real pleasure to welcome you to _____.

I know I speak for all the rest of your associates here when I wish you all the success, happiness and security in the years to come which you have visualized for yourself and your family.

We want you to know that we fully realize the responsibility imposed upon us by your decision to make your future with our organization. We will do everything in our power to help you in every way we can.

We're glad to have you with us! Good luck and our best personal regards.

Sincerely,

4

MODEL LETTERS THAT WILL SELL YOUR SALESMEN ON NEW POLICIES

4

MODEL LETTERS THAT WILL
SELL YOUR SALESMEN ON NEW
POLICIES

"Employees resist change!" It's almost a management cliche. Perhaps a cliche, but not a truth. Salesmen change the style of their clothes. They buy new cars, begin playing tennis instead of golf, change the style and length of their hair. Salesmen welcome change in their private lives and leisure activities. So why should they resist change at work? Maybe they don't resist change per se, but rather *resist being changed*.

But can't managers just order their salesmen to change and then watch the change take place? No, you can't order change—you must sell it. If you expect your salesmen to make the changes you request and to adopt new policies and procedures you must convince them that it is to their advantage to change. That's not so bad when you

63

stop to think about it. The sales manager's talent, his stock-in-trade, is persuasion. It's the same type of selling he enjoyed when he was back in the territory—and it can be as much fun.

1. ANNOUNCING A PRICE INCREASE AND SELLING THE BENEFITS

Oh, yes. The same old product that was a bear to sell last year at X dollars is now going to sell for X dollars plus 5% or 10%. Remember the feeling when you were a salesman? But the sky never fell, the customers never hung you from the highest light fixture as you were sure they would. As a matter of fact, at income tax time the next year it usually turned out that the price increase had contributed to a pleasant increase in commissions earned.

But somehow you forgot about that the next time a price increase was announced and the same doubts and fears recurred.

This is a tough one and worthy of an individual letter to the different types of salesmen on your staff. We'll look at a model letter aimed at the "comer" on your sales force, the guy who started to blossom last year and should be gaining confidence daily. A different approach is needed for the hard to motivate "average" producer on your sales staff (he lives conservatively and his wife works just so his income doesn't fall below "X" dollars). The hard nosed old pro who's going to retire in a few years (and he's been stashing it away for 20 years now) is a special case. He can make the difference in the national sales contest *when he wants to.* He can produce average sales working half days (and usually does). He turned down a promotion to sales management once because he "couldn't afford to take the cut." Many of his customers are better friends of his than you are. Now how are you going to get him to sell this price increase?

One form letter to all salesmen announcing the increase just won't cut it. This deserves a special approach to each type of salesman.

Model Letter 4-1

Dear _____

I do not claim that the new prices (price list attached) will make this year's selling easier than last year's. However, it is worth noting that if your unit sales this year are exactly the same as last year you will earn approximately $1,600 more in commissions just as a result of the price increase.

We are both aware of some favorable factors which will **(a)** result in improved unit sales this year. Our 8% price increase gives us an even greater advantage over our major competitor who just announced a 10% increase. Market conditions are improving almost daily in our industry, our customers are returning to their aggressive, expansion minded ways after last year's uncertainty—they're in a buying mood again!

The most important factor, I believe, is additional skill you **(b)** gained and toughness you showed in last year's adverse selling conditions. The $1,600 additional commission is automatic, I'm sure, and I know you won't stop there with just equalling last year's unit sales.

Sincerely,

Alternate Wording:

(a) This isn't our first price increase nor will it be our last. Let's consider for a moment what we have going for us that will help us to sell more despite the increase. To begin with there's the new model that represents all plus business. And our new adjustment policy has already proved to be a business maker. Finally, the new advertising program is bringing in new leads every day.

(b) Although price increases are unpleasant, I know from past experience you will make the most of the advantages you have at your disposal and will minimize the increase. That's the proper direction to take and the one that will insure that you will be enjoying at the very minimum that $1,600 increase in commissions at the end of the year.

Model Letter 4-2

Dear _____

This should be the year for each of us to reach new sales heights!

Our customers are in a buying mood again now that last **(a)** year's uncertainty is behind them. Our major competitor has just raised prices 10% across the board and I just got word that our new prices will be held to an 8% increase (price list attached). This means two things to you—your price advantage over competition just became even bigger than last year and you just got an increase of $1,200 in commissions earned if your unit sales remain the same as last year. But with the improved business climate in our industry and the even more favorable price advantage over competition, you'll probably increase your unit sales by 10% this year. And that means another $1,620 in commissions.

So use the advantages we've got going for us this year and make that additional $2,800 in commissions. We both know you can do it.

Sincerely,

Alternate Wording:

(a) The industry has just announced an 8% increase in prices effective the first of the month. We are following suit and I have attached a new price list. That means you will enjoy an increase of $1,200 in commissions earned if your unit sales remain the same as last year.

But since prices are a valid comparison only against what competition is offering for the same product, you can see that we enjoy the same sales advantages as before the increase. So there is every reason to anticipate that you will enjoy the same sales increase you planned before the price increase— only now you will earn more while getting your increase.

The price increase combined with your planned increase in sales will result in an increase of $2,800 in commissions. Sound great? You betcha. And I know you can bring it off.

Model Letter 4-3

Dear _____

You just got a raise, Ed. I've attached the new price list to this note. You'll notice that the increases have been held to

8%. That means your commissions earned for the coming year will increase by $1,400 on the same unit sales as last year.

Now I know you usually have figured out what the company is going to do before they give me the word. So you're probably as surprised as I am that the prices haven't been increased by 10%. You were probably counting on the additional $1,800 commissions you'd make this year with that price increase.

Well, our increase is just part of the news, Ed. Our major competitor just increased their prices 10% across the board.

So those accounts you've already got so solidly in your camp through the years of superb service you've given them are even more solid now with this wider price advantage. And I know while you were reading the past few lines of this note you already thought of another two or three accounts you've been warming up for a long time who won't be able to say no to the even bigger price advantage you can now offer them over competition. That should bring your increased commissions up $3,000 or more.

So, go get them. Sell quality and service and then use the price advantage for the clincher—just like you always do. I just wish I could be there to see how you do it.

Sincerely,

2. ANNOUNCING IMPROVED PRICES OR TERMS AND SELLING THE BENEFITS

When we have good news for our sales force we may sometimes feel the advantages are so obvious they don't require emphasis or explanation. When we fall into that trap we risk losing some of the additional business we would get if we used all of the motivational power contained in the good news. A simple explanation or announcement won't do when improved prices or terms are involved. Translate the improved prices or terms into potential sales increases. Use colorful cartoon letterheads where appropriate. Make it a celebration.

Model Letter 4-4

Dear _____

Get your prospect list out before you read any more of this letter.

Got it out? Now go through your prospect list and see how many "hot ones" you could close if you could offer them these terms:

Order Date	Shipment Date	Seasonal Savings Off List Price
11/15-12/8	12/31-2/28	5.5%
12/11-12/31	1/31-3/31	4.5%

Yes, we've finally got it! A cure for the "holiday put-off" and **(a)** the December "see me after the first of the year" blues!

We've got the closing tool we need to make December a season to be jolly—and prosperous! Let's use this sales tool to do just that. Let's not use it for an opener and give away our advantage in the close. We know that we have to sell the advantages of a big ticket product like ours before the discount will sway the buyer. But what an effect these terms should have on a lot of those buyers on your "hot list"!

We've got the extra edge we've been wanting. You know how to use it—so let's get out and make this holiday season a sales celebration!

Sincerely,

Alternate Wording:

(a)   Yes, we've finally got it! The discount that will make us completely competitive even with those few wholesalers that have been underbidding us.

What a tremendous tool this will be. Use it where you know price is the deciding factor. But don't give away profit (or commissions) unnecessarily.

(a)   Yes, we've finally got it! The closing tool that will make the most procrastinating prospect want to move now. What prospect can pass up the opportunity to make an extra 5.5%. And since he has to buy now to get the discount, it makes a perfect "reason to act now."

3. ANNOUNCING A TERRITORY REALIGNMENT

"If I had that piece of zone 4 that cuts into my territory I'd outsell John. That should be part of my territory. And that old section I've got down by the expressway—why those old buildings are mostly vacant and the few little mom and dad operations in there are losers. And the few office buildings left are full of answering services. They'll bulldoze the whole mess for 'urban renewal' one of these days and the whole section will be a vacant lot."

Sound familiar? The grass is always greener. Then you realign territories—and guess what happens? That worthless desert of urban renewal suddenly becomes a garden of eden to the salesman losing it and that neighboring piece of territory he's been lusting after for months doesn't look so hot when he finds out what quota comes with it.

Is there a way to convince all your salesmen that everybody wins and nobody loses as a result of the territory realignment? Individual phone conversations and face to face meetings may be called for to sell the benefit. However, written communication will be an absolute necessity to define the new boundaries, quotas and advantages of the change to each salesman.

Model Letter 4-5

Dear _____

You finally convinced me! You know that corner of territory 9 next to yours that you've mentioned to me several times? Well, it's now part of your territory. The northwest boundary of your territory is now the corner of Roosevelt Road (on the north) and Harlem Avenue (on the west) and the southwest boundary is on the corner of Harlem Avenue (on the west) and 63rd Street (on the south).

I've attached a new territory map and you'll notice all of the industrial area you wanted around the airport is included.

You'll also notice the old southern corner of your area has been made part of territory 8. I know you had two or three good prospects in that area and one or two good accounts. However, as you told me several times, a large portion of that corner consisted of parks, golf course and the college.

I've attached a partial list of prospects and accounts in the new section of your territory. This list is based mainly on John's old call report cards and certainly isn't complete. Let's meet at the office next Monday at 8:00 a.m. and go over the territory map with a cross reference directory and some of our prospecting tools and spend the rest of the day calling on several of the accounts and look the territory over.

The market index for that section is much higher than it was for the old section we transferred to territory 8. The quota is higher, of course, but you'll have no trouble exceeding it with the potential there. After looking at the figures, I can see why you've been wanting this area.

See you Monday at 8:00 a.m.

Sincerely,

4.   REDUCING A SALESMAN'S TERRITORY

"You break your neck to build up a territory, finally get everything rolling and making the good buck—and the so and so's cut your territory." Lines from "Death of a Salesman"? No. Lines from a salesmen's gripe session in the corner coffee shop, right? If you never said anything like that when you were a salesman, you're the exception.

They have a point though, don't they? That is how it looks sometimes from the salesman's point of view. But the salesman's territory isn't cut to limit his income. After all, the more he makes the more the company makes.

A sales manager may reduce the size of a salesman's territory because he's spending too much effort on a marginal area in the territory and too little effort on the most promising part, thereby lowering his production and income. Or he may reduce the salesman's territory because he's spending too much time driving and too little time face to face with prospects and customers—lowering his production and income. The manager may take an area out of a salesman's territory because the majority of the prospects and customers in that part are different from the bulk of his customers and he has consistently been unable to adjust to the different sales approach needed to create customers in that area. So a territory reduction is for the salesman's own good and he ought to welcome it rather than resist it.

I'm reducing your territory but it will result in increased sales and earnings for you." Again, remember how you would have reacted to that when you were in a territory. A salesman feels that his territory is his private property, his private preserve, his fiefdom. When you change the boundaries he will more likely react with emotion rather than with reason, similar to the reaction you would have if the town you live in told you they were going to build an expressway through your backyard for your own good. When the change in territory boundaries means a net reduction in area, you can't expect the salesman to be anything but disappointed, defensive and perhaps even hostile.

Your best persuasive powers are needed both face to face and in writing. The persuasion will be most effective if you have analyzed the territory with the salesman and discussed with him possible ways of increasing sales in the territory including the possibility of relieving him of the responsibility for covering the marginal areas so he can concentrate on the best potential.

If the announcement of a cut in territory size comes to the salesman in a letter with no prior discussion or consultation with him, there is a good chance he will take it as a personal insult to his abilities and become a real management problem for you.

Model Letter 4-6

Dear _____

I've given a lot of thought to the ideas we discussed last month. I agree with you that you've done a tremendous job in cracking the paper mills and related accounts in and around _____ city. I also believe you are right in anticipating even more new accounts and additional business from recent customers in that area. You definitely have found the key to that business.

I've also been going over your call reports for the last few months and some of my own notes to you regarding number of calls and accounts called upon. It appears I may have been getting in the way of your tapping the full sales potential of your territory. For instance, several times I asked why you hadn't called on _____ Company recently. A few weeks later I was questioning why the number of calls per day you were making had fallen off. After studying the map and remembering the roads in that part of the territory it seems to me I've put you in an unreasonable predicament. I've been expecting you to service the few old accounts over in _____ and bring in new business over there.

But the real business is in _____ city and surrounding areas. So I'm removing _____ from your territory and therefore freeing you from the responsibility of servicing the old, unproductive accounts down there. If we left the territory the way it was you would bring in additional business down there and increase the amount of your sales time there at the expense of bigger sales around _____ city.

You are now free to concentrate your sales efforts on the real mother lode. I'm confident your sales and commissions will increase. Give it Some thought and let's discuss your plans for really breaking it loose in the _____ city area when you phone in Monday morning.

Sincerely,

5.   ANNOUNCING A NEW PRODUCT

"If you aren't sold on your product you can't sell it to anyone else" is a time honored sales truism. When a new product is introduced the sales manager's first job is to sell it to his salesmen. A description of the features of the new product or service won't sell the salesmen. They'll get that from the brochures and sales aids provided. What will it do for their prospects and for them? The emphasis must be on the sales opportunity.

Model Letter 4-7

Dear _____

This is our day!

With everything we've got going for us right now—what one **(a)** addition to our product line would you like to have to make this the perfect sales situation?

You told us. Back in November at the annual sales meeting, what did you ask for?

You've got it!

The _____ Super Shuttle Feeder opens sales opportunities with that large group of prospects who require a center loading feeder.

This is the saleman's dream—all the market conditions right and the home office heard your request for the product you need to put it all together!

You've got it!

The time is right—the product is right—the *price* is right (see attached).

This is the situation you've dreamed about. A starter supply of brochures is attached. Order blanks are attached. Send them back filled in!

We know this new product is the key to record sales in a perfect market situation. You invented it—you've got it— enjoy it and sell!

Sincerely,

Alternate Wording:

(a)   After nine months of research and field testing, here is a new product with proven customer need and appeal. In our initial field test, 84% of the customers surveyed reacted favorably to the benefits of our new Super Shuttle Feeder. Fifteen of them wanted to place orders immediately.

6.   ANNOUNCING PRODUCT MODIFICATIONS

When you announce a change in the product line or modification of existing products, it will more likely be welcomed if communication like this precedes the change.

Model Letter 4-8

Dear _____

The time is rapidly approaching to begin work on the 19____ model lineup. As you well know, _____ has long relied on dealers to a large extent for ideas to help formulate our model line, and with economic conditions as they are today it is very important that we have a line that will be very saleable next year.

Since you and your salesmen are on the firing line 100% of the time, you are best equipped to provide us with information on what is needed right now to maximize sales. We will appreciate your help with answers to the following questions, plus adding any thoughts you have:

1. What new models are needed for 19____?
2. What equipment changes should be made on the 19_____ models?
3. What color changes or additions should be made next year?
4. What models should be dropped?
5. What items of equipment make certain models more saleable than competition?

Please check with your salesmen to get their thoughts and please also pass along your own ideas on the 19____ models.

Thanks for your help.

Sincerely,

An announcement of product modification should stress the inherent market opportunities and refer to the part the sales force had in suggesting the change—if this is the case.

Model Letter 4-9

Dear _____

In response to requests from many dealers, Silver Mist will be available on the following models effective immediately: Continental models 320, 322, 324 and 326 and Sprint models 422 and 424. Sky Blue will be added to model J38-9 and J38-6 Sting Rays.

These additional colors on Continentals, Sprints and Sting (a) Rays should enhance sales considerably.

Sincerely,

Alternate Wording:

(a) Our market research work has confirmed your feelings that the customer wants a greater color selection in our product line. So here it is. Use it to get that sale that is sitting on the fence.

7. ANNOUNCING A NEW SALES AID AND SELLING THE BENEFITS

If the salesman doesn't believe the new sales aid will help him make the sale, you can bet it won't—because the prospect will never see it.

An efficient and worthwhile sales tool won't necessarily sell itself. Be sure your introduction tells how to use the sales aid most effectively and points out types of sales situations where the sales tool applies.

Model Letter 4-10

Dear _____

A powerful new sales aid is now available. It is an owner testimonial record bound in a jacket printed with hard hitting sales messages. To produce the record, on-farm interviews were made with enthusiastic owners in 10 different states—Pennsylvania, New York, Michigan, Indiana, Illinois, Wisconsin, Minnesota, Iowa, Kansas and Oklahoma. Each 8-inch record is recorded on both sides with 10 minutes of dairy testimonials on the front and 10 minutes of beef information on the "flip side."

The record is narrated by _____, well known farm broadcaster. On both the dairy and beef sides, a number of points are made in the actual words of owners. Less labor, lower field losses, better livestock production . . . all these points are made again and again backed up with actual owner experience. The record is bound in an attractive folder which contains additional information about _____, including tax advantages and reasons to "buy now." It comes in an envelope suitable for mailing.

Here is what we recommend you do:

1. Become familiar with the contents of the record and jacket.

2. Mail a record to your best prospects. Then schedule a follow-up call with each prospect to discuss how the prospect can enjoy the benefits of _____ farming referred to on the record jacket and by _____ owners on the record.

3. When a first call reveals a qualified prospect, leave a copy of the record for the prospect to play prior to the next scheduled contact.

4. Use the record at fairs to get new prospects. Play the testimonials over a public address system at your display. Announce that the record is available to those who request it. Record request cards can be distributed for follow-up.

You will want to start using this new sales aid right away. The record is available for immediate shipment in lots of 100 at $ .50 each. Tapes are available of the record for your use at fairs in cassette form or reel-to-reel at $1.50 each.

Sincerely,

Here's an additional letter which introduces a sales aid through a dealer organization. Notice how it uses the dealer as a valuable link in the communication chain.

Model Letter 4-11

Dear _____

Hogs are beautiful—about $20 more beautiful than they have been in the past.

Attached is a copy of the new _____ *Swine Feeding Handbook*. The new feeding handbook will be mailed to your salesmen August 6.

You may wish to discuss the new feeding handbook with your salesmen in a dealership sales meeting soon after that date. We have attached five feeding problems and the solutions, if you wish to include a practice session in using the tables in the handbook to fill animal nutritional requirements in your sales meeting.

Notice, too, that tables 3 and 4 provide examples of typical diets. We believe this handbook contains all of the information your salesmen need not only in conventional sales situations, but also anything they might need when it gets tough and complex.

Your salesmen can provide a valuable service to their customers and increase sales by using this sales tool.

Sincerely,

5

LETTERS TO WRING EXTRA DIVIDENDS FROM YOUR SALES CONTESTS

5

LETTERS TO WRING EXTRA DIVIDENDS FROM YOUR SALES CONTESTS

The success of any sales contest is due in large part to the amount of excitement and enthusiasm generated. The awards for winning contribute to that excitement. But no contest will be completely successful without an abundance of communication to inform, motivate and reward all participants. A proven way to get the job done is with well written and imaginative letters.

The sales contest consists of three phases: the launching in which rules and awards are announced, the work phase and finally the payoff. Each phase makes its own demands on the sales manager who desires to motivate and guide his men. The model letters that follow are organized in these three categories for your convenient use.

Many sales managers like to use prepared letterheads for their contest letters. These may be prepared specifically for the contest with contest name and slogan printed. Envelopes can also be imprinted with matching identification. The idea for such identification on envelope and letterhead is to command the salesman's immediate attention and to inform him that something special and important is underway. If your budget won't permit the investment in special letterheads for the contest, try the prepared type you can purchase.

Make it a policy that during a contest, no letter will be sent to your salesmen without some type of illustrative material to lend showmanship and color. Salesmen are generally men of action. Reading a detailed letter may not be one of their favorite activities even when it involves a chance to win money. We have omitted the illustrations in our model letters because such illustrations must be closely tailored to the situation, but we have suggested where appropriate types of illustrative material would be useful.

1. ANNOUNCING THE SALES CONTEST

Whenever possible use a special meeting to kick off a sales contest. Such special attention provides the contest with the sense of importance and excitement required for salesman enthusiasm. But that is not always possible, is it? Your sales force may be so widely scattered that bringing them all together to announce a contest would require all or a major portion of the contest budget. Or perhaps, as many sales managers do, you run contests on a rather continual basis, making a meeting-type kick off impractical. Then letters are an excellent way to launch the contest. Each of the following letters was used for that purpose. Although the incentive and rules of the contest may vary from what you have planned, you will find considerable value in the various letters to build interest and impact to your own announcements.

Model Letter 5-1

Dear _____

HERE IS YOUR THREE MONTH
SPECIAL ACHIEVEMENT BONUS PROGRAM.   **(a)**

This is the contest that provides chances for really outstanding money. You can reach figures amounting to many hundreds of dollars with this bonus—it's up to you!

As a special consideration, we'll apply your winnings to travel, to the gifts of your choice, to gift certificates to the store of your choice, or to cash money!

During this bonus contest last year, Bill Holland won a trip to Ireland. Jack Spencer won a mink stole for his wife. Jerry Ebring wton $600 in cash.

This year the awards are bigger. The chances of big winnings are even greater. And with all we've got going for us this year, everyone can be a big winner.

Details of the contest are attached. Take special note:

- The contest awards are large than last year.
- Goals are based on the same percent increase as was used last year.
- There is a special grand bonus for the top salesman in each product line.

As usual I'll be mailing progress reports every week. Don't wait until the last minute to qualify for this great money making opportunity.

Starting date: Noon, Friday May 30

Ending date: 9:30 am, Friday August 29

Sincerely,

Alternate Wording:

(a) TRY YOUR HAND AT SWEEPSTAKES POKER

For one month only (June), we'll be playing poker. Every Model 630 sale will entitle you to play one poker hand. Every Model 830 sale will entitle you to play two hands of poker. Every 960 sale will entitle you to three hands.

Hands will be played each Friday based on sales that week. I'll provide the pot which will consist of 1% of sales made divided evenly among deals played.

The writer of this letter used illustrations of playing cards to add interest to his announcement.

The following letter takes advantage of the extra impact the salesman's wife can provide to make a contest a success. If she becomes involved in the contest, she can encourage her husband to greater achievement. Moreover, she is likely to be tolerant while he devotes the necessary evenings to the extra work required.

This particular letter displays a generous understanding of human nature. One caution, your own knowledge of your salesmen and their wives should be applied in using this powerful letter. While this device should work extremely well with most salesmen, there may be some family situations where you would not want to use it. Applied with thought and discretion it can spark the most productive contest you've ever had!

Model Letter 5-2

Dear _____

I know you'll be pleasantly suprised to receive the three checks for $100 each which are made out in your name and enclosed with this letter. The only disappointment is that they aren't yet signed, but let me assure you they soon will be if everything goes according to plan.

The checks are all part of a contest in which your husband is now taking part. You see, each month he meets his quota for the next three months, I will personally sign one of the checks for you to spend as you wish.

I'm sure ___(salesman's name)___ is going to be able to make **(a)** his contest goals but if you would like to help him here are some suggestions:

1. Encourage him when things are looking bad. Gray spots are bound to appear. Give him that pat on the back and encourage him to make his second effort.
2. Show your understanding when he has to work extra hours to bring off the tough sale.
3. Help him off to a fresh, fast start every morning. His whole day depends on it.

With your help you and I both know he can do what he has set out to do. When he does, the three checks are yours.

Sincerely,

Alternate Wording:

(a) Why would we involve you in a contest such as this? We are convinced you are an important part of your husband's success. Only you can provide the home that will permit him to concentrate on his sales effort. Only you can provide the encouragement when things get rough. And only you can be his sounding board to help him work out the rough spots in his sales presentation.

You can just bet that every winner of this contest will have his wife solidly behind his efforts.

The writer illustrated this letter with a proliferation of money and checks around the border.

The following model letter introduces an incentive program that caters to the salesman's need for ego satisfaction by using the ever popular trophy.

Model Letter 5-3

Dear _____

The enclosed photograph was taken last year as our salesman of the year ___(name)___ received the traveling trophy from our company president ___(name)___ at our annual awards banquet. This same picture, you will recall, ran in the newspaper and in the company magazine with an accompanying article.

Who's going to be the winner this year? Will it be _____ again or will a dark horse pull out to win it? Perhaps one of the previous year's winners will come back as a two-time winner. At this point, every one of you is a likely candidate.

You will be pleased to know that the award will be made in Honolulu this year. That's right, you and your wife, if you are the winner, will be flown at company expense to receive your award under the swaying palm and gentle breeze. The attached sheet provides the details.

OK, all you beach bums. Let's get with it. One of you is going to be a winner.

Sincerely,

If you have other sales managers working for you, consider including them in the contest. They can make a big difference to the success of the contest and too often they are neglected. This letter was written for that purpose.

Model Letter 5-4

Dear _____

Here's something on the side especially for you! We realize how important you, the sales manager, are to the success of any incentive program. When you put your shoulder to the support of any effort, things begin to happen.

So when your sales team reaches goal, you will receive a .5% bonus on all sales. When you reach 110%% of goal you will receive .75% bonus on all sales. And should you be successful in reaching 120% of goal you will receive a full 1% bonus on all sales.

Are the opportunities for big money available to you? What do you think?

% of Quota	Here's What You Will Earn
100%	_____
110%	_____
120%	_____

The rules are simple. Just meet or break quota. The contest ends midnight, July 31.

Sincerely,

2.   THE WORK PHASE

Most contests suffer from the seventh inning lull. Enthusiasm wanes. Extra effort declines. To maintain that first week enthusiasm requires periodic letters that inform contestants where they stand, that prod the low men, hold out the carrot a little further for the leaders, and provide new ideas for reaching sought after goals.

This first letter was written to the salesmen that were trailing in the contest.

Model Letter 5-5

Dear _____

What would you do with an extra $350 next month? That's what your share of the contest winnings would come to if you are a winner in the *Over the Top* contest.

Can you do it? Consider this:

—You're already half way there. Since less than half of the contest period remains, you would need about six average sized sales to make it over the top. That should be a very possible endeavor—just two sales each week.

—Others are reaching goal. Three salesmen are already winners. Four more are within 10% of going over and will surely make it within the next two weeks. That only proves it can be done.

—You were able to make it last year. Are conditions different now?

In fact, *I'm sure you can make it.* I'm so sure that I made a little side wager with V.P. Marketing this morning. He indicated his concern that you wouldn't be able to go over the top during the contest so I bet him $50 that you would— that's how sure I am. How about it? Can you prove me right?

Sincerely,

The following letter was also written for the slow starter, for the salesman who is lagging behind the remainder of the pack.

Model Letter 5-6

Dear _____

Here is the latest in contests—The Great Turtle Getaway **(a)** Break. No, it didn't start out with that name but our few slow starters are bound to make it that.

You have yet to get out of the gate, John. And I know you better than to believe you are satisfied with that. Big winnings are at stake, not to mention your standing in the sales force.

But there's still plenty of time. Remember the tortoise and the hare?

Sell your shell off!

Sincerely,

Alternate Wording:

(a) Turtles seldom win anything. It took a fairy tale for one to win a race against a rabbit.

It's time for the turtles to get out of the gate, John. There are big winnings at stake and I know you better than to believe you are satisfied with your present standing.

The sales manager who wrote the above letter included a toy turtle with the friendly barb. It undoubtedly served as a constant reminder to the salesman.

Don't neglect the leaders of the contest just because they are ahead of the rest. This letter was intended to spur a contest leader to even greater accomplishments.

Model Letter 5-7

Dear _____

It's great to see your name in first place on our contest board **(a)** in the sales office.

Right now you'll want to take all precautions to make sure it stays right there. Watch out for the slogan "Number 2 Tries Harder." Bill Wright is just behind you and closing. Can he catch you before the contest ends? Do you have a couple of extra sales you can bring off in the last ten days?

Don't slow down now! I'll bet you can taste and smell those sea breezes off the coast of Acapulco already.

Sincerely,

Alternate Wording:

(a) But most races are won or lost in the final hundred yards. Now's the time to follow-up on that referral you put on the back shelf last week. Now's the time to give that procrastinating customer one more try. Now's the time to take that doubtful prospect on a tour to a user installation.

How effective you are in these last 10 days will make the difference.

If you market through dealers, this letter will be useful. It is actually a pair of letters—the first designed to motivate the dealer, the other the dealer's salesmen.

Model Letter 5-8

Dear _____

Bob, Dave and I just want to take a moment to thank you for your efforts in starting the "Getting Your Share" program off to an excellent start. With your leadership we know *(Name of Dealership)*   will be getting its share *plus*. We have enclosed a letter to all of your employees. I hope you will post it or copy it for each.

Sincerely,

Model Letter 5-9

To All Employees:
  (Name of dealership)

We just want to thank each of you for the fine results you have shown during the first three weeks of the "Getting Your Share" sales contest. Your sales are right up among the best of them.

The idea of "Getting Your Share" is that if you give a little you will get a little more and that's a fact. "Getting Your Share" is for all of you. We know that all of you will get your share as you all continue the team work and cooperation you have demonstrated to this point in the contest.

Sincerely,

The salesman is likely to be very receptive to new ideas during a sales contest, especially if he is trying to catch the leader. This letter takes advantage of the receptivity of this special period.

Model Letter 5-10

Dear _____

Here it is the third week of the *4th Quarter Blitz* contest already. And if you're like most of us, you are looking around at this point for new ideas that will help put you over the top.

Here's an idea. Don't overlook referrals. You need all the **(a)** help you can get when you're trying to get new leads. Referrals multiply your efforts. They can give you additional ears and voices. Make the most of them.

For example, don't overlook:

- Present customers. Ask every one of them for a lead.
- Shoppers. Even if they don't buy, they may be willing to provide a good prospect.
- Centers of influence. Shopkeepers, doctors and others in the area who meet a lot of people may be willing to provide you with leads.

Make the most of referrals. They may make you a winner.

Sincerely,

Alternate Wording:

(a) Here's an idea. Use demonstrations on every sales call. Demonstrations give impact to your presentation. Your prospect will remember only about 20% of what you tell him but he will likely remember as much as 80% of what you demonstrate to him. Demonstrations get the prospect involved, especially if you have him perform part of the demo. Demonstrations give meaning to your words.

You have many ways of demonstrating your products. Use the ball demo. Or the puncture test. Use the acid demo. Pick the most appropriate to demonstrate what your prospect needs to know, but use at least one on every call.

It's these little differences that will win the contest.

The last week of the contest requires special fanfare. Send a letter every day as you work to the climax. Send letters special delivery to demand attention to the program. Send telegrams or mailgrams. Here is an example.

Model Letter 5-11

TELEGRAM

5 DAYS LEFT IN 1775 OR BUST CONTEST. ALL TALLIES CLOSE. ANYONE A WINNER. IT COULD BE YOU. AN ADDITIONAL $2550 COULD DO IT.

Or, for the salesman in the lead:

Model Letter 5-12

TELEGRAM

5 DAYS LEFT IN 1775 OR BUST CONTEST. YOU ARE IN LEAD BUT ALL TALLIES CLOSE. NEED ADDITIONAL SALES NOW TO INSURE YOUR VICTORY.

The sales contest encourages healthy competition among salesmen. You can further this competitive spirit with the letters you send. Here is an example.

Model Letter 5-13

Dear _____

Although Harry Bresson is a little behind you in the current *Go For Broke* sales contest, he seems to think he is going to take the lead away from you in the next week or two. As a matter of fact, he told me exactly that just yesterday.

I felt it was only fair to get your direct reaction. (Holding your ears, Harry?)

I'll turn my head if any side bets are in order.

Sincerely,
cc: Harry Bresson

3. THE PAY-OFF

When the contest is complete, one final letter remains—to announce the winners. This is a good model of such a letter.

Model Letter 5-14

Dear _____

Congratulations. You are a winner in the "Extra Effort" sales contest. The results for each salesman and what he has won is provided on the attached sheet.

All considered, the "Extra Effort" has been a tremendous success. Sales have increased during the contest period by 35%, making it one of the best sales thrusts ever. This success has been possible thanks to you and the superb "Extra Effort" you gave to bring in those extra $_____ in sales. We couldn't have done it without you. Thanks!!

Sincerely,

6

GETTING SALESMEN ON YOUR TEAM DURING TOUGH TIMES AT THE HOME OFFICE

6

GETTING SALESMEN ON
YOUR TEAM DURING TOUGH
TIMES AT THE HOME OFFICE

Remember your days as a salesman? Stop remembering that great, beautiful sale. Instead remember those two quarters in a row when the company seemed bent on ruining you. Remember? You'd promise delivery and it wouldn't happen. Something was wrong with everything. Quality control was out to lunch. Service didn't exist. You had to make every sale two or three times. Even your best customers were beginning to doubt you. Tough getting up in the morning, wasn't it?

And what did the home office tell you? "Problem? There's no problem. Our product is the best, our service is best. All we need is some real selling from you guys out there."

The futility of this ostrich-head-in-the-sand approach has become increasingly evident. Today there is a new breed of salesmen who expect straight talk from sales management, who expect to have a voice in the management of their territory, and who expect the company to back them up with quality products and service.

Sales managers today recognize the futility of pretending all's right with the world when the company is facing a delivery crisis, product shortages, or product and service quality problems. These managers realize that salesmen are among the first in the company to become aware of such problems. They also recognize that salesmen are capable of dealing effectively with problems.

Salesmen generally are not asking the company to solve all problems within twenty-four hours. Rather, they want to know what the situation is, what general approach management expects them to follow during the crisis, what specific methods they are expected to use and what end results they are expected to achieve if these things differ from previously agreed to plans. Salesmen, by the very nature of their daily activity, are more familiar than anyone in the company with the effect the company crisis is having on the customer. Sales management should therefore invite the salesmen's participation in continuing efforts to improve the situation. Immediately useable pragmatic solutions might result.

Telephone communications are vital to the line manager during such problem times. But written communication provides extra impact to remind both salesmen and sales manager of the goals and procedures agreed upon.

These are difficult letters to write. Any negative, defeatist tone in the correspondence is deadly and can be counted on to produce a morale problem in the sales force. But an unrealistic "there's no problem" tone can have an equally devastating effect. The model letters that have been included in this section provide a positive approach to the problem at hand while:

1. Recognizing the situation or defining the problem.
2. Explaining the general approach the company expects of the sales force during this period.
3. Making specific assignments to salesmen.
4 Inviting salesman participation in continuing efforts to improve the situation.

This section is organized according to the types of home office problems you are likely to encounter. Each section provides not only a letter from the sales manager to his salesmen, but an additional letter from the general sales manager to his line managers. As you will note, the problems and communication approach is different for each.

1. EXPLAINING DELIVERY DELAYS AND EMPHASIZING POSITIVE SALES APPROACH

Making the sale is tough enough under ordinary circumstances. But when a salesman has done all the hard work of making the sale and late delivery forces him to make the sale over again a second or even third time, morale is bound to be affected. If sales management knows delivery delays may continue for a period of time, communication with the sales force is necessary.

Model Letter 6-1
(From the chief sales officer to line sales managers.)

Dear _____

As you know, delivery delays have recently become a factor in our selling. The production people are working to correct this situation.

Their efforts will undoubtedly produce improved delivery in the near future. However, I believe it is realistic to take probable delivery delays into consideration in our marketing plans for the next six months.

From a marketing standpoint I am determined that we   **(a)** achieve three main objectives in the next six months:

1. Maintain our largest and most profitable customers. We are establishing an allocation and priority system (details sent under separate cover) to insure that competitors do not gain an advantage with our established accounts.

2. Continue to gain new key accounts. The priority system will provide for orders from new key accounts.

3. Gain orders for future delivery and accustom our customers to this kind of planned and organized purchasing. Customers incentives (discounts) are provided in our allocation and priority system to encourage this planned approach to purchasing which will benefit both our customers and us.

Take the following steps with your salesmen within the next two weeks:

A. Explain the delivery situation is temporary and will begin to improve shortly, but the problem will not be completely solved for approximately six months. Do not be apologetic and do not place blame on "those production people." This situation is partly due to successful selling by your salesmen and a high quality product. Success, growth and expansion often bring problems such as delivery delays. There is no need to fix blame, but there is a need to convince your salesmen that this is a "good problem" which need only be a minor irritation as they continue to increase their sales and their incomes.

B. Explain our three main marketing objectives— maintain volume of major accounts, gain new accounts, sign solid orders for future delivery rather than immediate delivery.

C. Reach agreement on specific goals with each of your salesmen in each of these areas. Use an incentive contest among your salesmen based on meeting and exceeding these goals or any other device you wish.

D. Invite suggestions from your salesmen which will help accomplish our three main marketing objectives for the next six months.

I expect a report from you within two weeks outlining your specific goals for your sales office in each of the three main marketing objective areas.

I realize emphasis on large, profitable accounts will be necessary to reach our goals and we may miss some business from smaller marginal accounts during this crucial period. But we can continue our sales growth during the next six months and be in an even stronger position in each sales territory when delivery capability returns to normal six months from now.

I know your salesmen will view this period as a time of sales opportunity if we clearly present the job to be done.

Sincerely,

Alternate Wording:

(a)   Your sales organization must provide the greatest care to communicate with your customers during this period. Customers will accept delivery delays only when they know to expect them and know when to expect their end. This means your salesmen have a special job during the next six months to keep our customers fully informed of the progress of our delivery situation and to inform them what they can do to minimize the impact of such delays.

When the line sales manager has received a definition of the problem and clarification of the general approach of the company to the situation, he can communicate with his salesmen. Certain definite action and results are needed from the salesmen. "Informing" them is not enough. They must be convinced that the action they are instructed to take is in their own best interest and will result in maximum sales and income for them under present circumstances. Face to face meetings with the salesmen individually or in groups will be necessary. Two-way communication; discussion of the situation, the activities they are to perform, the results they must produce; is a necessity. Just informing the salesmen risks silent disagreement and resistance from them. A cynical, defeatist attitude in the sales force will be disastrous. This letter was used to prepare them for the face to face meeting.

Model Letter 6-2
(From the line sales manager to his salesmen.)

Dear _____

As you know, delivery delays have recently become a factor in our selling. The production people are working to correct this situation and their efforts will undoubtedly produce improved delivery in the near future. This situation is due in large measure to your effective selling and our high quality product. It is a good problem that often accompanies growth, expansion and success.

The vice-president of marketing has set three major objec- (a) tives for the next six months—maintain our largest and most profitable customers, continue to gain new key accounts, gain orders for future delivery and accustom our customers to this kind of planning and organized purchasing.

To help us reach these objectives, an allocation and priority system for orders will be instituted immediately. A customer incentive or discount program is also being introduced immediately to enable us to sign orders for future delivery. In other words, we are being given the sales tools we need to maintain our fast pace.

We will have a meeting at the office next Monday morning to discuss these new sales tools and plan for their effective use.

Please prepare for our meeting by reviewing your present customers and prospects. Be prepared to list your key accounts and key prospects. Also think about how you can use the customer incentive program to sign orders for future delivery and which accounts will be most receptive to this program.

Sincerely,

Alternate Wording:

(a)   During the next six months we must maintain our largest and most profitable customers, continue to gain new key accounts, gain orders for future delivery and accustom our customers to this kind of planning and organized purchasing.

Model Letter 6-3
(From the chief sales officer to line sales managers.)

Dear _____

As you know, orders for our recently introduced sprayer model _____ have been coming in at a rate even higher than we anticipated. Our customers are recognizing and clamoring for the built-in advantages that our three-way mixing ratio sprayer provides.

Demand has been so great we are having difficulty filling all orders. One part, supplied by a particular vendor, is in short supply and we do not presently have an alternate source. I anticipate the shortage situation will continue for at least ninety days.

I am pleased with the reception this product has received in   (a) the market and concerned at the possibility of losing sales due to short supply. However, I'm not sure that we must lose sales. Several other products in our line will perform a similar function to the model _____ although I recognize that they do not include some of the features of this model.

I suggest you emphasize to your salesmen the need to determine from the buyer exactly what application he requires and then ask themselves what alternative products in our line will do that job. I must concede that in some situations only our model _____ would satisfy the customer. In those situations the salesman must convince the customer that the model _____ is worth waiting for and make the sale on a back order basis.

I believe your salesmen will get the job done. In the meantime, our production people are doing everything they can to catch up with the demand.

Sincerely,

Alternate Wording:

(a) We have initiated an emergency order system to take effect immediately. It works like this. We are holding back a small stock of sprayers to supply dealers who are completely out of stock or are in immediate danger of running out. In those situations we will draw from our emergency stock as long as it lasts.

> Five units is the maximum order we can honor for delivery from emergency stock. I'm sure you realize that this system won't work if it is abused. It is designed for the true emergency condition. If your salesmen order out of the emergency stock for regular stock replenishment, the supply will soon be depleted.

> To secure stock from the emergency supply your salesmen should mark their orders "Emergency Stock."

Model Letter 6-4
(From the line sales manager to his salesmen.)

Dear _____

I remember thinking one day after a sales call on a particularly hard nosed prospect, "I wish the day would come when sales were so good that he couldn't buy my product no matter how badly he wanted it!"

Well, that day seems to be here with the new model _____ and it isn't fun like I expected it to be. I know you feel the same way.

The recently introduced sprayer model _____ has been selling as well across the country as it has here. A vendor supplied part is in short supply and a back order situation has developed. I've been assured that the factory people are doing everything they can to catch up with demand, but for the present we are in a back order situation.

However, our sales don't have to suffer. There are at least **(a)** two things we can do. We have a unique, high quality product superior to anything competition can offer with this new model. We should be able to convince the buyer that it is worth waiting for rather than buying from competition. Also, we can work harder to determine from the buyer exactly what application he requires and then ask ourselves what other products in our line will do that job. I suspect in many cases we will find that we can satisfy the customer's requirements with one of our products. You know, our sales of several other models have fallen off since the model _____was introduced.

Let's get together Monday and discuss it. You've got some ideas on keeping sales as high as they've been, I know.

Sincerely,

Alternate Wording:

(a) We can maintain our high level of sales by convincing the buyer that our product is worth waiting for. We can also do a better job of determining exactly what function the product will perform and then ask ourselves what other products in our line will do that job.

2. EXPLAINING SERVICE PROBLEMS AND EMPHASIZING POSITIVE SALES APPROACH

When it becomes clear that customers aren't getting the attention and quality work they have become accustomed to from the service department, it is time for action. Your salesmen will demand to know how you are correcting the situation and how to sell while the situation is being corrected. They are not concerned about who is at fault. The following letters tell the sales force what action the company is going to take and what action the salesmen are to take.

Model Letter 6-5
(From the chief sales officer to line sales managers.)

Dear _____

You and your salesmen are right. Our service capability has fallen behind the sales force. Customer complaints are evidence that immediate action must be taken to bring customer service up to an acceptable level.

The service department manager has promised to hire additional servicemen and buy additional modern equipment for faster and better quality work on each service call. Also, he is beginning a training program on servicing the newest products for all service personnel. Please communicate these improvements to your salesmen.

We are setting up a hotline system to minimize customer problems during the period it will take to get service back to the high level we all expect. The purpose of the hotline system is to prevent any customer from having his production shut down because he can't get service from us. The details of the plan are attached. Note that we have divided service calls into four categories. Those situations which could give us a black eye in the market if mishandled receive top priority. Explain this system to your salesmen and be sure they know how to use it with their customers. If the salesmen cheat and attempt to get top priority service assistance for routine service problems, the program will fail and they and their customers will be the ultimate losers.

Finally, I think it is appropriate to remind your salesmen that if there were no problems there would be no need for salesmen. We fell down momentarily in the service area, but we are taking steps to get back on top of it. During the interim period the salesmen will have to recognize valid service problems when confronted with them by customers, learn to use the hotline system to greatest advantage to minimize customer dissatisfaction and be confident in the knowledge that the situation is temporary and being corrected.

We remain open to any additional suggestions you or your salesmen may have. Let me know next Friday how your salesmen react to the service improvements which are coming and how well you feel they are using the hotline system.

Sincerely,

In response, a sales manager wrote this letter to his salesmen.

Model Letter 6-6

(From the line sales manager to his salesmen.)

Dear _____

The General Sales Manager has just informed me of action **(a)** being taken right now to improve speed and quality of service. Additional servicemen and equipment are just part of the improvement. I'll describe all of the steps being taken when we get together on Monday morning.

We are also putting a procedure into effect to insure that no service problems occur which could give us a black eye in the market. Please review your accounts and identify any service problems which you consider crucial. Put the details of each situation in writing—keep it short—and be prepared to discuss them with me on Monday. I will describe a hotline system to insure customer satisfaction in crucial service situations when we meet.

We fell down momentarily in the service area, but we are getting back on top of it.

While the service improvements are being implemented we have to recognize valid customer service problems when confronted with them, learn to use the new hotline system to greatest advantage, and be confident in the knowledge that this temporary situation is being corrected.

If you have any additional suggestions for keeping customers happy while the service department improvements are being implemented, I'd like to discuss them when we meet on Monday.

Sincerely,

Alternate Wording:

(a) You and I are very sensitive to the need for good service with our customers. I'm happy to tell you that the home office is just as sensitive to the need as we are. They, too, have sensed the recent slipping in the normally high quality of service we provide.

To remedy the problem they are expanding the size of the service department. They are also adding additional equipment so that service response time should be reduced considerably. I'll describe all the steps being taken when we get together on Monday morning.

3. ANNOUNCING CUTBACKS IN SERVICES

Management is sometimes faced with a choice between increasing prices or cutting back popular extra services. Particularly in times of inflation and rising costs, cutting back services may be chosen as a lesser evil than a price increase. This action is usually taken to keep the product competitive or, in other words, to help the salesman. However, the salesman may not appreciate the "help" unless he can quickly see the advantage to him and his customer. These letters announcing cutbacks in service stress the positive benefits.

Model Letter 6-7
(From the chief sales officer to line sales managers.)
Dear _____

Material and labor costs have been rising rapidly in our industry. We have considered an across-the-board price increase. However, we feel an increase is undesirable at this time from a competitive standpoint.

The only alternative is to reduce costs. We are therefore **(a)** eliminating the first service call which we previously provided the customer at no charge.

I believe your salesmen will prefer the elimination of the no-charge first service call to a price increase. Please communicate this policy to your salesmen so that they understand the advantage to them and to their customers.

Sincerely,

Alternate Wording:

(a)   The only alternative is to reduce costs. Beginning November 1 we will no longer be able to provide the no-cost layout service as previously. Such a policy puts us in line with the remainder of industry. A recent survey indicated we are the only company which provided this service at no charge. By eliminating the no-charge service we can maintain our price and keep our salesmen in position to meet all competition.

Model Letter 6-8
(From the line sales manager to his salesmen.)

Dear _____

We've been wondering when the price increase would come. Well, we can stop wondering. The home office just informed me there will be no price increase! I think you'll agree this is the best news we've had in quite a while.

Material and labor costs have been increasing and a reduc- **(a)** tion of cost is necessary to enable us to hold the price. The first service call which we previously provided the customer at no charge has been eliminated. I think you'll agree it's a good deal.

I suggest you make a call on new customers approximately thirty days after delivery. If you feel minor adjustments are called for, you may wish to sell the customer on a service call. A little extra effort after the sale will pay dividends, so let's keep the customer happy and maintain our competitive price.

Sincerely,

Alternate Wording:

(a)   Material and labor costs have been increasing and a reduction of cost is necessary to enable us to hold the price. As a result, effective November 1, we will no longer offer a no-charge layout service as in the past. Although no-charge layout service has been an advantage we have all been able to use, I am sure you will agree that remaining competitive price-wise is a much greater advantage.

The price schedule for our layout service is attached. You will find it is very competitive with other companies offering a similar service.

Occasionally a service is no longer necessary or is no longer economically feasible-and must be dropped. The communication should point out that the service is no longer needed and make it clear that its elimination should not affect sales.

Model Letter 6-9

Dear _____

We have been informed by _____ Refrigeration Company that effective the end of next month they are discontinuing installation of air conditioners.

Most of our vehicles are now available with factory air conditioning. Many of you have already made local installation arrangements with air specialty shops or have trained people to do your own installations.

While initially the elimination of this service may cause some inconvenience, the need for it has become minimal and more practical alternatives have replaced it. Therefore, we are not planning to provide an installation service to replace _____ Refrigeration Company.

Some of the dealers who have a number of trained people may be interested in installing units for other dealers. If this is the case, please let me know and we will publish a listing of dealers who would be willing to provide such a service.

Sincerely,

7

LETTERS THAT CORRECT POOR PERFORMANCE WITHOUT LOSING A GOOD MAN

7

LETTERS THAT CORRECT
POOR PERFORMANCE
WITHOUT LOSING A
GOOD MAN

Every sales manager has the responsibility for correcting unsatisfactory salesman performance. Handled properly, it is an extremely rewarding responsibility. But many traps lurk for the unwary. If the sales manager becomes angry as he corrects the salesman, the salesman is likely to become angry in turn. If the manager becomes vindictive, the salesman will react by becoming defensive. Sugar coat the correction and he salesman will likely miss the point. Ignore the problem ane it only grows.

Attempting to resolve a performance problem without first understanding its cause is much like trying to put out a fire without first knowing what is feeding it. You can very easily make conditions worse by applying the wrong solution. Correcting salesman performance involves a bit of manager sleuthing to determine why the salesman is behaving as he is. Does he know how to perform as you desire? Does he have the know-how but lack the will to perform? If he lacks the will to perform what causes it to exist? Answers to questions such as these will determine the type of corrective action that will be most successful. Determining the cause of salesman behavior problems is a subject in itself, The point is that the solution you provide must be tailored to the cause of the problem.

Some performance problems, by their nature, require personal handling. For example, if a complex solution is required, such as coaching the salesman to handle a special type of sales approach, or if the prodlem is of a personal nature such as a drinking problem, personal handling is certainly in order. There remain, however, many instances in which a letter is most efficient and economical. And even when a personal correction is required, a letter is desirable as a follow-up to fix points of agreement and to ensure that agreed upon action is taken.

Both types of letters are provided in this section. Where personal contact is likely to be more effective, we have so indicated and have provided a follow-up letter that has proven valuable in nailing down the points agreed on in the meeting.

1. SUGGESTING MORE SALES CALLS

Successful sales results are unlikely if the salesman is just not making enough calls. The possible causes for such a problem are several. The salesman may not realize how many calls are required to get the job accomplished. He may be involved in outside activities so that sufficient time to make the required number of calls is impossible. He may be unwilling to change from his present ineffective habits. Each cause requires its own letter.

This first letter is designed to inform the salesman who is unaware of the number of calls necessary to get the job done.

Model Letter 7-1

Dear _____

Selling is something like a funnel. You can't expect to get more out the bottom of a funnel than you put in the top. In selling you can't expect to get your quota of sales until you make calls on an adequate number of prospects.

While examining your call reports this week, I came up with **(a)** these interesting facts. You made 120 calls on new prospects last month. On the average you made five new prospect calls to get one sale. And each sale you made averaged $525. With a little simple pencil pushing you can easily see that to meet your quota for the coming months you must: increase the dollar sales per customer, reduce the number of calls per sale or make more calls on new prospects. Perhaps a goal to achieve all three is too ambitious, so let's concentrate on making more calls on prospects as a starter. It's probably the simplest to achieve and will show the quickest results.

To reach your sales goal this month would require five additional calls on new prospects each week. Possible? I'm sure you will agree that it is. In other words, you can continue to sell with exactly the same efficiency that you are currently enjoying and merely call on five additional prospects each week and your sales goal is within reach.

Would such a step up in sales effort be worthwhile? Just con- **(b)** sider the added bonus that is yours when you reach your quota. Or ask your wife what she would be able to do with the added income. It's within your reach—all that's necessary is one more new prospect call each day.

Sincerely,

Alternate Wording:

(a) One sale usually requires about five calls on new prospects. This is fact based on the experience of other salesmen. An average sale in our coniany is $500. Using these figures you can easily see that you must plan to make about 125 calls per month just on new prospects to make your quota. Compare these figures with your own experience. It can make a good yardstick to determine if you are feeding enough into the top of the funnel to meet the goals that you have set.

What would it take in the way of additional calls to make your sales goal this month?_____ more sales calls each week? Would it be worth that to you and your family? I'm sure you will agree that it is.

(b) Would such a step up in sales effort be worthwhile? Well, it could easily put you in top running for winning the current sales contest. It's within your reach—all that's necessary is a small increase in the number of new prospect calls you make each day.

(b) Would such a step-up in sales effort be worthwhile? Well, it could easily put you in position to win the salesman of the year award. Let me know by the 15th of this month how you plan to approach this opportunity to improve sales. I'm sure you can make it pay off.

This next letter was written to a salesman who the manager felt knew that more sales calls were necessary, but who had fallen in a complacent rut that made additional sales calls distasteful.

Model Letter 7-2

Dear _____

Have you noticed the red flag that's showing on your call reports— The flag is the definite slowing of number of calls you are currently making as compared to last year. Based on past experience, you can expect a drop in sales to follow close behind.

I know you want to maintain the good sales record you have **(a)** going this year. So now is the time to look to the basics such as the number of calls you make each day. Why don't you develop a plan right now that includes bringing the number of calls you make up at least to the number that you made this time last year. **(b)**

Let me know what you come up with.

Sincerely,

Alternate Wording:

(a) I know you will want to qualify for the incentive trip to Bermuda this fall. So now's the time to eliminate all the possible sales problems that may get in the way.

(b) The remedy involves just some determined planning. Some time each weekend jot down the names of prospects you plan to call on during the coming week. Compare the number with the average number of prospects you called on last year. If the figure does not equal or exceed last year's average, include some additional prospects. Only through careful attention to your prospecting will you be able to beat last year's sales.

I'll be watching your call reports closely to see how you are progressing on this important part of your job.

2. SUGGESTING CALLS ON LARGER ACCOUNTS

Many salesmen have worked diligently to oblivion by concentrating their efforts on smaller, relatively unproductive accounts. Many salesmen begin their sales career working with smaller accounts because the competition for these accounts is usually less. But the amount of effort for the return is often great and, as the salesman's experience broadens, he will usually seek the larger and more profitable account. But what about the salesman who, like the child who clings to his baby-like ways too long, won't grow to the larger account? In resolving this management problem the sales manager must search out the cause. Does the salesman fail to realize the importance of the larger, more productive account? Is he reluctant to break away from selling the small account that provides his security? Each of the following letters approaches one of these problems.

Model Letter 7-3

Dear _____

If you had the job of filling a dump truck with sand, would you rather use a bucket or a power shovel? In a similar manner with sales, the larger the account, the quicker the quota is reached and the greater the earnings. Although the larger volume account may be a bit more difficult to secure, the returns make it a highly profitable effort.

Here's just one example. In a field analysis conducted a while (a) back, we learned that the $5,000 per year account requires about forty hours per year to sell and service. The $50,000 account requires about 100 hours per year. That makes each hour spent on the larger account 400% more profitable.

You will find the same ratio holds true in your territory. Concentrate on identifying and selling the larger prospects—

those with $30,000 or more annual potential. That doesn't mean you abandon the smaller accounts you have now. Only as you sell new accounts, put more of your time on the larger prospect. The net result to you will be not only more sales and greater commissions, but an easier sales job. Remember, research proves that it takes less effort per sales dollar to sell the large account than the small one.

Sincerely,

Alternate Wording:

(a) Doesn't it stand to reason that selling the larger account requires about the same number of calls as selling the small account? Granted that you must often sell "smarter" on the larger account, especially if your prospect is a specialist in his area. And then, too, you may find that your competition is greater for the larger account since more salesmen are interested in the larger profits to be made there. As a result, you might not be able to sell as large a percent of the bigger prospects, but past experience indicates that the net result will be more total dollar sales for every hour invested.

Here is a model letter for the salesman who has fallen into the comfortable habit of calling on the smaller account even though he is aware of the more profitable larger account.

Model Letter 7-4

Dear _____

Here's a firm offer for an extra $200 for the first account you land that buys over 16,000 units per year. Why am I willing to put such money on the line? Well, for one thing the larger account is worth more to the company. But even more important at this point is to give you the incentive to go after the larger account.

We've talked about this before, and since our last discussion I have been reviewing all the possible "reasons" other salesmen I have worked with have given for not calling on larger accounts. Here are the major ones:

1. Selling the larger account requires meeting with committees.
2. Locating the right man to sell is more difficult.
3. Because the man you are selling in the larger company is a specialist, the salesman must know more about his product and its application.
4. When you miss on a large account you lose out on a large investment of time and effort. Missing a smaller prospect doesn't represent such a large investment.
5. Selling the small potential account represents a comfortable area of selling. I know the accounts and how to approach them. I have a proven track record there.

Does one or more of these reasons dovetale with your own?

As we have discussed previously, each of us must get a balance of accounts. You can little afford to put all your time and effort on the small account. Such effort will only limit your sales success, your earnings income and your future with this company.

Here's a little evening task that will help both you and me. **(a)** Take a few minutes to write out why each of the reasons for not selling large volume accounts is a fallacy. Send your written thoughts to me by next Tuesday. Then, perhaps, we can discuss them some by telephone.

Here's to that first 16,000 per year account.

Sincerely,

Alternate Wording:

(a) At our sales meeting next Monday we are going to discuss the fallacy in each of these reasons to sell exclusively to the small account. Would you please be prepared to take about five minutes to discuss point number three. Some of the other men are doing the same with the other points.

Here's to a profitable meeting next Monday.

3. REQUESTING THAT THE SALESMAN SEND IN REPORTS PROMPTLY

Few salesmen like to complete reports. It would seem as though the aptitude to complete reports is at the opposite pole from the aptitude for working with people. But the fact remains that few salesmen excape the detail part of their jobs. And many sales manager must cajole, threaten and continually remind their salesmen to complete and submit their reports.

Those sales managers who have been successful in getting reports completed and submitted when due have found that the solution lies with impressing on the salesman how he stands to benefit from completing the report. Forget why the report is important to you, the sales manager. Instead tell the salesman what's in it for him. That is the approach used by this model letter. The sales manager who submitted it indicates he has had considerable success with it.

Model Letter 7-5

Dear _____

Yes, Sales Call Reports are important to this office. But that is the least reason for completing them regularly. The important reasons are those that are important to you. Other salesmen have told me that their call reports are worth an additional $5,000 per year to their incomes. Here's why.

The Sales Call Report provides the means for planning your sales activities. It reduces wasted calls, helps you to reduce needless driving, helps you pinpoint exactly what you intend to accomplish on each call.

When you complete your call report immediately after making the sales call, you are better able to determine how well you were able to accomplish what you intended. A sustained record of your calls helps you determine if you are making enough of each type of call and where to increase your emphasis.

The Sales Call Report is a working tool that benefits you in another way. By sending in your call reports weekly, I am able to compare your experience with the other salesmen to determine how you might further improve sales. In turn, you are able to communicate your good experiences to the other salesmen for their assistance.

So complete your Call Reports every day and send them in to this office every Friday evening. It's worth at least $5,000 per year to you.

Sincerely,

4. PREPARING THE SALESMAN FOR A COACHING LESSON

No sales management responsibility is more important to the orranization or to the salesman than on-the-job coaching. Where coaching has been an on-going activity, the salesman is likely very receptive to the boss's visit. But the salesman is likely to approach his first coaching experience with suspicion and fear. In his view, the boss may be there to spy or find fault. His reaction is to keep the boss from learning what is really transpiring in the territory. So he takes him to those accounts where little opportunity exists for the manager to coach the salesman's activities.

Successful coaching depends on proper groundwork, begins with a letter ahich announces the meeting, and describes what the salesman can expect and how he will benefit. We selected this letter from among several as that which accomplishes its purpose most effectively.

Model Letter 7-6

Dear _____

My present plans involve meeting with you on Monday and Tuesday of next week. I would like to ride with you as you make your regular calls on accounts. Don't plan anything out of the ordinary. Just make those calls you would regularly make on those days.

As we make calls together, perhaps we can both benefit, I may be able to pick up some sales pointers that the other salesmen can use. In turn, perhaps you will be able to get some ideas that others have found valuable.

Although I'll be accompanying you on every call, I will not be entering into the sale itself. Then after the call, perhaps we can discuss some cf the things that happened and why.

Based on the reactions of the other salesmen that have already been involved in this experience, I believe you will find our time together rewarding. The other salesmen have told me:

1) They have been able to learn new sales approaches. For example, Bill Bolden was able to find an answer to an objection that has caused him considerable problems in the past.

2) They have been able to get a fresh approach on a particularly tough prospect. I won't join in to help you sell the tough customer, but I may be able to give you an unbiased and fresh insight into the problem. That has happened on three occasions as I worked with the other men.

3) They have been able to identify problem areas that have previously escaped them. Often we are so close to the problem that we fail to see an obvious solution. Or perhaps we have fallen into costly habits that we are totally unaware of.

I am looking forward to the meeting with you on Monday. I'll see you in your office about 8:30 ready for a busy day.

Sincerely,

5. CORRECTING THE SALESMAN WITH A MONEY PROBLEM

The salesman who has difficulty nanaging his finances can not only be an embarrassment to the company, but can create unnecessary administration problems and financial risks to the company. If the salesman's money problems are due to his ignorance in handling money matters, this letter is of value.

Model Letter 7-7

Dear _____

I'm very sorry to learn about the difficulty you have encountered on your home purchase. Transfers are difficult enough without having things like this occur.

There is a cardinal rule in buying a home that would have helped you avoid this type of problem—always get a title search before agreeing to purchase a home. This precaution will uncver the types of faulty titles you are having a problem with. There is undoubtedly a major title insurance company in the area. Look at the yellow pages or check with a local broker.

In the meantime, what to do with your present situation. **(a)** You indicate your down payment is tied up which precludes your buying another home until the present deal is resolved in court. We can probably get approval on a 5% interest down payment loan from the company to get you another home here. Approvals will require about 24 hours. Repayment can be made when you get settlement on your court suit. Let me know what you want to do.

Sincerely,

Alternate Wording:

Right now your biggest problem is how to get a home in the area so you can move your family here. We can be of some assistance here. The company would be willing to act as guarantor on a bank loan to provide you with a down payment for a new home loan. Let me know if you want to pursue this possibility.

Here is a letter that is intended to correct salesman performance where the salesman has gotten into financial trouble because of immaturity and a lack of discipline. Because of the personal nature of this type of problem you should seek your initial discussion on a personal basis. But after the personal discussion you should send to the salesman a letter that summarizes the points made and the agreed upon solution.

Model Letter 7-8

Dear _____

Our meeting yesterday was, I believe, rewarding to both of us. Not only did it help me to understand your problem more clearly, it provided the basis for a successful solution.

Your current job problems are due to personal money problems. Several gambling debts have put you into a position where you have been unable to meet your obligations. The worry has carried over into the handling of your job.

As a result of our discussion, you have agreed to stop all **(a)** gambling. Further it is agreed that on any further evidence of your gambling you will be suspended for a period of ten working days.

As we discussed, you will contact one of the local family financial advisors to assist you in working out a solution with your creditors and to work out a family budget. I will expect the advisor to inforn me that he has established a working relationship with you.

These are stern measures, I realize, Jerry, but this is a very serious problem. If I can personally be of assistance or if the company can assist, let me know immediately. I can help only if you let me know.

Sincerely,

Alternate Wording:

(a) As a result of our discussion, you have agreed to stop all gambling. In addition you have agreed to contact each of your creditors to arrive at a mutually satisfactory solution to your overdue debts. I expect you to send me a note regarding each account to advise me of the solution you have reached.

6. CORRECTING THE SALESMAN WHO REPORTS IN SICK TOO FREQUENTLY

The salesman who misses work because of reported illness can be a delicate problem. If he is truly ill, the situation may be beyond his control and of significant concern to him also. But what if he habitually uses illness as an excuse to pursue more attractive activities?

The first step in handling this type of problem is to provide the salesman the opportunity to explain his absences. Many sales managers handle this step by telephone, seeking an explanation each time the salesman is absent. The following letter seeks an explanation by letter only after the salesman has been absent from work a number of times. When it is used is a matter of management preference and the closeness with which the sales force is controlled.

Model Letter 7-9

Dear _____

Probably nothing is more disconcerting to you than the necessity for missing a day's work. Most of us feel that we are in some way shirking our responsibility. This concern makes a legitimate illness all the more difficult to bear.

Your call reports indicate that you have been ill on three different occasions each of the past two months. A record of illness such as this is certainly beyond the ordinary. I know it must be of concern to you.

Your absence is also of concern to me. In the first place I want to be of assistance to you or your family should you be encountering some difficulty. Second, your illness represents a significant loss to the company in sales and in customer good will.

Can I be of assistance? **(a)**

Sincerely,

Alternate Wording:

(a) If you have not had a physical to determine the nature of your problem, I would strongly urge you to. In the meantime, can I be of any help to you and your family?

Many sales managers have become increasingly aware of the problems of overweight among their salesmen. For the sales force continually on the road, eating every meal in a restaurant and getting little exercise, this is often a problem that robs many productive years from the salesman and the company. Here is one sales manager's answer to the problem.

Model Letter 7-10

Dear _____

Here's a challenge that may be a life saver. Medical authorities and the insurance companies are continually impressing on us the importance of weight to the health of the heart. Heart disease remains the number one killer in the United States.

As I looked around the sales meeting the other day the impact of the problem fell hard on my awareness. I'll bet at least three-fourths of us are ten pounds or more overweight (and that includes me). If the statistics hold for this group of men (and there's no reason why it shouldn't), there may be some of us who won't be around ten years from now to brag about our paunch.

That's the reason for this little incentive. For every pound you take off and keep off for a period of eight weeks, the company will pay you $10. (For some of us there's gold in them thar' hills.) The weighing in cermony is at next week's sales meeting. Exactly eight weeks from that day we will have the payoff (after another weigh-in, of course).

How about a little side wager. I'll bet I can beat any of you in pounds lost in the next eight weeks. Any takers?

Sincerely,

7.   CORRECTING THE MOONLIGHTING SALESMAN

The salesman's job freedom sometimes provides him the opportunity to engage in outside activities that sap his time and efforts. He may endeavor to sell a sideline product along with his primary sales effort. Or he might take on an evening job that tires him and detracts from his full time job. Most companies discourage their salesmen from moonlighting. Such a problem can usually be resolved with a well conceived letter such as the following.

Model Letter 7-11

Dear _____

As you may be learning, selling for _____ is more than a full time job. Experience has taught us, and I'm sure it will you, too, that it is just impossible to sell two lines at the same time.

As you probably sense, I am referring to your present efforts to sell not only the _____ line but a sideline as well. Here are just two of the difficulties you are likely to encounter:

    1)   You will not have enough time to sell both lines effectively. Selling a second line requires added time

for locating and qualifying prospects, making an explanation of the line to the prospect, servicing, setting up displays, answering complaints and problems. Clearly since your position with _____ requires your full time, any added activities will only detract from the performance of your job.

2) Any problems you should encounter with your sideline (such as supply, quality, service, etc.) will surely have a negative impact on our products. Our customers do not hold a clean distinction between our products and others you may handle.

Problems with the sideline become too easily associated with our products.

You can easily see why it is our policy that no _____ (a) salesman carry any other line in addition to his regular _____ line. The company permits no exceptions to this policy. To do so would lead to problems and to limited sales effectiveness. Let me know by Friday what you intend to do about your second line.

Sincerely,

Alternate Wording:

(a) In the interest of the company and our customers, no one is permitted to carry a second line of products. If this leads to some complication of which I am unaware, let me know. Otherwise I will expect that you will drop the second line immediately.

This letter was written to a salesman who had a part-time job that detracted from his sales efforts.

Model Letter 7-12

Dear _____

I have received a request in the morning's mail indicating (a) that you are considering a part-time job working evenings

and Saturday in addition to your job with _____.
Although other salesmen with _____ have occasionally
attempted part-time work, few of them have ever been successful. Most of them will tell you a part-time job does not
permit a successful career. Why? First, because your sales job
isn't an 8 to 5 job. As you are aware, there are times when
you must work evenings and weekends to bring off that important sale. A part-time job will surely limit your ability to
provide each customer with the service and attention he requires for complete satisfaction.

In addition, your evening and weekend work will surely im-
pair the energy you need for successful performance of your
job with _____. This lack of vitality may not be readily
evident to you because of your youth. But as the weeks and
months pass, you will surely feel the drain. Unfortunately the
loss will be primarily to your job with _____.

The decision is yours to make. And as you consider this im- **(b)**
portant juncture in your career, I hope you will consider my
counsel. Let me know about your final decision.

Sincerely,

Alternate Wording:

(a) You mentioned the other day that you had taken a part-time
job to help pay for the medical bills while your wife is preg-
nant. Although I can understand the economic pressure that
leads to such a decision, consider these problems that often
arise for those who pursue the course you have chosen. To
begin with, your job isn't an eight to five job. As you are
aware, there are times when you must work evenings and
weekends to bring off that important sale. A part-time job
will surely limit your ability to provide each customer with
the service and attention he requires for complete satisfaction.

(b) The decision is yours to make. In reaching the right decision,
you must weigh the immediate gains of more cash in the
pocket with the more long term advantage of your career
with this company. Your present course will certainly
jeopardize the long term.

8. CORRECTING THE SALESMAN
WITH TOO MANY OUTSIDE INTERESTS

Salesmen are usually naturally gregarious. Joining organizations may be a personally rewarding activity and frequently provide leads for additional sales. But for the salesman who has difficulty saying "no," joining can be a problem. They join more and more organizations, and take on even more responsibilities within the organizations to which they belong. As they become more involved in these outside activities, their jobs may suffer. The sales manager may have to supply the discipline the salesman lacks. Here is a letter that undertakes that function.

Model Letter 7-13

Dear _____

Here's a way to say "no" in three languages:

    "nyet"   "non"   "nein"

I learned them from my wife. She knows how to say "no" in 101 languages.

At some time or the other we all find it difficult to say "no." But sometimes it's very necessary. Take clubs for instance. If you said "yes" to every club or office offered, there would soon be no time for anything else.

And that brings us to the point of my letter. I don't know of every club and office you take part in, but I know of enough to question the time you invest. Have you been finding yourself at luncheons that drag on into the afternoon? Have you found it necessary to take care of organization business during working hours? Have you occasionally found that club affairs were creeping into your thoughts when you should be concerned with business? All these are symptoms of the need to say "no" more frequently.

If any of these symptoms fit your situation, learn at least these three ways to say "no." I can provide more if needed.

Sincerely,

9. WORKING WITH THE SALESMAN WITH A DRINKING PROBLEM

The salesman with a drinking problem provides the sales manager with one of his more difficult management tasks. To ignore the problem is to invite loss of time on the job, company vehicle accidents, poor customer relations and limited sales. Reasoning and discipline are generally of little value. So widespread is the problem that almost every sales manager has encountered it at least once.

The personal nature of the drinking problem makes it one that is best discussed face to face. As soon as you suspect that the salesman's work is suffering because of his drinking habits, call him in to explore the problem and to work out an agreement to resolve it.

A letter is frequently useful as a follow-up to the meeting. Because of the addictive nature of his drinking habits, the salesman will often promise to make corrections and then slip back when he returns to territory. A letter encourages the salesman to take the action he has promised by putting the agreement in writing.

Here is a follow-up letter one sales manager wrote to encourage one of his salesmen to follow through with his promise.

Model Letter 7-14

Dear _____

I would like to express my appreciation for the frankness with which you were willing to discuss your alcohol drinking patterns at our meeting.

To recall some of the main points of our discussion:

1. Drinking to excess creates job problems. Among the more important is time lost on the job. You indicated that you have lost several days in past months because of alcohol intake.

   Driving constitutes a second problem. Driving from one account to another with even a small amount of alcohol intake constitutes an increased risk—for you, for others on the road and for the company car. You indicated that on occasion you have been drinking while on the job.

The third problem is the effect your drinking has on your job performance and on the customers you serve. Alcohol dulls the senses and cripples your work efficiency. Not only are your job decisions second best but your customers undoubtedly sense they are not getting the service and care they deserve.

2. You acknowledge the problem and promise to combat it. Your first step is to contact a member of Alcoholics Anonymous to join that organization. I have provided you with the name and telephone number of a local member. **(a)**

3. I have agreed that you will continue in your present position on the condition that you join the Alcoholics Anonymous group and follow their instructions. **(b)**

This is an important crossroads you face, John. The decisions and actions you take in the next few weeks will determine your future welfare and that of your family. Many others have faced the same problem and won. You can too. I'm pulling for you and know you can do it. Let me know in a few days what progress you have made.

Sincerely,

Alternate Wording:

(a) You acknowledge that you have something of an alcohol problem but that you feel that you can handle it without outside assistance. You have promised that you will not drink while on the job and that you will not permit alcohol to interfere with the performance of your work.

(b) I have agreed that you may continue in your present position. However, we agree that we will meet weekly to review your progress in handling this problem. Any indication that the problem is persisting will require more stringent solutions.

8

SALES MANAGER'S LETTERS THAT LOCK IN THE SALE

8

SALES MANAGER'S LETTERS

THAT LOCK IN THE SALE

Buyer's Remorse! Ever encounter it? No matter how good a sales job your salesmen have done, the customer may reflect after the salesman has departed to ensure he has made a good decision. He may begin to question whether a competitor's product might have been more appropriate or if he should have acted at all. Many a sale has been lost because the sales department felt its job was done when the prospect said "I do."

A timely letter will often ward off "buyer's remorse." Such a letter seeks to reinforce the customer's decision to buy your product and to assist him in deriving the greatest possible satisfaction from its use.

1. CONGRATULATIONS ON YOUR PURCHASE

One way to reinforce the buyer's decision is simply to tell him he has made a good decision and that he will be happy as a result of what he has done. These letters accomplish this objective.

Model Letter 8-1

Dear _____

Thank you for your recent order. It is always a pleasure to do business again with a valued customer.

I hope it means that our team of sales people, office staff and service and rental personnel understand you and your organization and are delivering our product to you in a way and at a price that is comfortable for you.

Please continue to take advantage of the many ways in which **(a)** we can assist you and feel free to call me whenever I may personally be of help to you.

Our goal is to merit the right to do continual and increasing business with you.

Thank you again for your recent order.

Sincerely,

Alternate Wording:

(a) We aim to deliver not just a product but to deliver the benefits it will produce for you. Our service and technical staff is available to provide advice and assistance to be sure you get the full benefit of the product.

If your product or service is of the type that is purchased for future use rather than an immediate necessity, you are probably particularly concerned about heading off "buyer's remorse" and reassuring the buyer of the wisdom of his purchase.

The sales manager who wrote this letter knows the value of following up after the sale and reassuring the buyer.

Model Letter 8-2

Dear Mr. and Mrs. _____

Your foresight and consideration for your family are clearly proven by the enclosed agreement covering a Family Memorial Estate in _____ Memorial Park.

Your Memorial Counselor joins me in assuring you that in years to come your family will appreciate the wisdom of this move and recognize that you made a sound investment in many respects. I know it will give you deep personal satisfaction and peace of mind to have taken this step, and I earnestly hope no occasion will arise for actual use of your family estate for many, many years.

Sincerely,

Model Letter 8-3

Dear _____

Your decision to stock the _____ line of hair dryers puts you on the sales team with over 1600 other retailers across America.

Bill Martin, your Sales Representative, and I join forces to assure you that your decision has been a wise one. The experience of those 1600 retailers tells us you can expect rapid customer acceptance of the _____ line due to our extensive advertising program. The engineered quality and quality control steps ensure complete customer satisfaction and a minimum of adjustment and service problems. Finally, our pricing policy will provide you with a significant profit contribution to your business.

Welcome to the _____ team!

Sincerely,

In some lines of business after the sale support is particularly important. The writer of this letter believes the retailer needs to be reminded of the backup he receives from the manufacturer along with the quality products he buys for resale.

Model Letter 8-4

Dear _____

Thank you for the courtesy you showed our representative _____ the other day and for your order.

Enclosed are advertising slicks to help you in the development of promotions. I know _____ left a kit of promotional ideas and materials with you. He told me you had several ideas for advertising and promotions and thought these slicks would also be of help.

Don't hesitate to get in touch with _____ or me if you have any questions or need additional assistance. Our job is to make selling our product a profitable pleasure for you.

Sincerely,

Model Letter 8-5

Dear _____

Thank you for the opportunity of getting together on Monday.

I was sorry to hear you are having difficulty moving our model _____ and am cancelling the balance of your order for that model as you requested. As we agreed we will work with you to merchandise your present inventory of 200 cases. Al will be calling on you next week to suggest a promotion used by several other dealers which resulted in a high **(a)** level of sales. Al will also discuss an order for the other _____ products which you mentioned would retail well in your area.

Your willingness to work with us is most appreciated, and we will put forth our best effort to earn this confidence.

Sincerely,

Alternate Wording:

(a) If, after thirty days of using this promotional plan you still have inventory, we will accept it with no freight-back cost to you. In that event, Al will get proof-of-delivery from you so we can issue credit and invoice the new customer.

2. SELLING ADDITIONAL SERVICES AND PRODUCTS

Present customers are sometimes prospects for additional products or services. The salesman may uncover potential uses for other products in your line or you may be using a "shotgun" approach to contact your entire prospect list.

Model Letter 8-6

Dear _____

At the suggestion of our representatives Mr. _____ and Mr. _____ I am writing to offer further information concerning our Alloy Line of cap screws.

The Grade 8 Alloy Cap Screws which we supply meet or exceed all SAE and ASTM standards as well as Military standards for Grade 8 Threaded Fasteners. A chart is attached which shows the physical characteristics of our product.

The extra effort our service people make to insure on time delivery and accurate shipments is built in when you place an order with us. The understanding of your special requirements which our sales representative has acquired in serving you insures the extra effort you have come to expect from us.

We trust that this is the information which you require, but if **(a)** there is any further data which we can supply, please feel free to call on us at any time.

Sincerely,

Alternate Wording:

(a) Our representative _____ will be calling on you shortly to provide any additional information you require and to determine if this product fits your particular situation.

Model Letter 8-7

Dear _____

Congratulations on your purchase of _____. You are now the owner of the finest appliance made and can look forward to years of enjoyment.

This quality machine will serve you for years to come. It has been designed to require minimum maintenance. We suggest a yearly checkup to allow a qualified technician to make minor adjustments and insure that this fine appliance remains in like new condition. A brochure describing our service program is attached along with a service agreement. We hope that you will sign the agreement and return it to us and allow us to keep your fine appliance performing at peak efficiency for years at a very modest cost.

Sincerely,

Model Letter 8-8

Dear _____

We value your business and would like to extend credit privileges to your company. The benefits of being the holder of a _____ Credit Card are:

- You can receive a discount on our regular rates.
- The need to carry cash for rental deposits is eliminated.
- The _____ Credit Card frees you of finance charges.
- As a member of the _____ family of credit card holders you will receive V.I.P. service.
- Ease case flow problems that tie up valuable funds.

To become a _____ National Account complete the application and return it to me in the enclosed envelope as soon as possible. Thank you.

Sincerely,

Model Letter 8-9

Dear _____

Looking for that added profit opportunity? Here's an important one that will fit in with the _____ line you are now marketing.

This new product has all the features required to be a successful direct mail product. The price is right, it is a quality product, it is aimed at the expanding "do it yourself" market, it is UL listed, it has a better price point. A catalog page is enclosed.   **(a)**

Our representative _____ will be calling on you next week to explore the potential of this product in your market.

Sincerely,

Alternate Wording:

(a) This new product has all the features you look for in a self-service store product.

Model Letter 8-10

Dear _____

It's been a good year for you and your company. Increased sales and profits were rare in a tight economy and competitive market.

Although many elements were undoubtedly involved in your company's performance, I'm sure we are agreed that your imaginative use of our service was one contributing factor.

I believe you can contribute even further to your company's success by utilizing another of our services. We can now provide a low cost, low paper work system that will help you to effectively manage all of your receivables, reduce your days' sales outstanding, and improve your cash flow.

Dave will contact you next week to explore how this system might fit into your operation.

Again, my sincere compliments on your personal accomplishments and your company's outstanding performance during the past year.

Sincerely,

9

LETTERS THAT OVERCOME THE CUSTOMER'S RESISTANCE TO CHANGE

LETTERS THAT OVERCOME THE CUSTOMER'S RESISTANCE TO CHANGE

The sales manager must be alert for the tendency to resist change. His customers present an especially acute problem, because if they resist the changes he must initiate, they can easily take their business elsewhere.

But some change is necessary even if the customer does resist. Prices must change. Marketing policies change. Products change. People change. And since you can't eliminate the change, you must carefully prepare your customers to make the transition as painlessly as possible.

Any change is an opportunity to contact and sell old or existing prospects, present customers or existing accounts. The communication should stress a new opportunity provided by change in your company or product. Involving the salesmen and getting their suggestions for both the points which should be stressed in the letter and who it should be sent to will strengthen this approach. Also, the salesman should receive a copy of the letter before it is sent to the prospect or customer. These letters can be important sales tools leading to sales when changes occur.

1. ANNOUNCING THE PRICE INCREASE

Perhaps the most commonly encountered change in today's age of inflation is the price increase. Probably every sales manager has written at least one and probably many such letters. Unfortunately, many such letters are cold and impersonal announcements on a take-it or leave-it basis.

Most really effective price increase letters have three common elements:

1. They stress the company's efforts to hold the line on prices;
2. They review the pressures that are at hand;
3. They stress areas where the company has been successful in containing prices.

Model Letter 9-1

Dear _____

In the past one and one-half years, we have been able to hold the line on prices with only one price adjustment on our _____ line. In the past six years we have been successful in avoiding all mid-season price adjustments. As you can guess, this was no easy accomplishment.

This year, we have been forced to give way on a limited (a) number of price adjustments if we expect to maintain uninterrupted service. Otherwise we would not be able to continue to provide top quality parts in these lines. Even now we have been able to hold the price line on 80% of our line through innovations and cost reductions.

The attached price list reflects the lines where changes are necessary. We will continue to honor all orders received before March 15 at old prices.

Please get in touch with our Representative or with me if you have any questions or need assistance.

Sincerely,

Alternate Wording:

(a) We will continue to hold the price line on 80% of our products this year through innovations and cost reductions. On the few products where small increases were necessary we continue to provide top quality at a competitive price.

Model Letter 9-2

Dear _____

No one in the sales profession reacts favorably to price increases. I realize that includes our valued distributors. But, as you know, the continued pressure of upward prices is hitting everyone—including us. We have been able to spare you price increases on several occasions during the past 18 months by tightening our belt and by finding new and more efficient ways of getting the job done.

Now we have come to the point of either a price adjustment or lowering product quality. We have come to the conclusion that you would rather that we increase prices than jeopardize your markets with an inferior product.

Effective October 1, prices on all products will be increased by 8%. Any orders received before that date will be invoiced at present prices.

Just a sales note. A price increase can make a strong reason for your customers to act now. "Stock up and beat the price increase" is a story your sales reps might make big profits with.

Sincerely,

2. SELLING THE DISCOUNT RESTRUCTURE

Changes in quantity or price discounts can result in customer reaction similar to those encountered with price increases. Unless the plan is decidedly in their favor, resistance is likely. To sell such changes requires highlighting the benefits of the change to the customer.

Model Letter 9-3

Dear _____

As we discussed by telephone, I can certainly appreciate your desire to have available a cash discount option.

We have provided cash terms in the past, but discontinued the practice when many customers began taking unearned discounts.

As a result, some needed shipments were held up until invoices were settled and, in general, an unpleasant condition was encountered.

Our solution was to reduce the prices on all our products by 2% and to eliminate the cash discount. In general our customers have reported satisfaction with this arrangement and it certainly has eliminated the problems previously encountered.

Thank you for bringing the cash discount option to our attention. Periodically we review our policy in this matter, and we will certainly take your preference into account on the next such review.

Sincerely,

3. PRODUCT DISCONTINUANCE

The discontinued line can be a problem. It no longer is profitable to continue marketing the line due to its small volume. On the other hand, a few dedicated customers continue to use it. The ideal solution is to switch them over to another product that is comparable and that will provide essentially the same satisfaction. But since the customer may be reluctant to change, it may take a careful application of human relations to keep him buying.

Here is a letter that does the job quite well.

Model Letter 9-4

Dear _____

First, I wish to thank you for your frequent purchases of _____ over the past years. It's the loyalty of _____ and other companies like yours that provides us with substantial satisfaction.

Although thousands of customers have bought _____ over past years, we now find that present sales do not warrant continued production. Although manufacture is being discontinued, we still have a moderate stock to serve your needs.   **(a)**

We understand the importance of _____ to you. So may we offer a replacement that, we feel, will provide even greater satisfaction. The attached catalog sheet describes our recommendation. I have highlighted with a yellow marker the plus features of this product. The added investment is only slight as you will notice.

_____, your Sales Representative will be calling on you within the next few days to answer any question concerning the use of this recommendation.

Thank you for your continuing orders.

Sincerely,

Alternate Wording:

(a) We don't believe in change just for the sake of change, however. We would like to suggest a replacement which we feel includes the capabilities you appreciated in _____ and provides additional features as well.

4. INTRODUCING A NEW SALESMAN

Nowhere is the constancy of change more evident than in the assignment of personnel to sales territories. If your organization is very large, new salesmen are continually being assigned. Here, too, the sales manager must be alert to possible frictions with the customer who has grown comfortable with his present sales representative and who resents the change.

Model Letter 9-5

> Provide photograph
> of salesman here.

Dear _____

We are pleased to announce the appointment of Mike _____ as your new Sales Representative.

During his six years here at _____, Mike has worked **(a)** in our service, rental and sales departments gaining valuable technical and practical experience. You will find Mike not only highly qualified to serve your needs, but also a friendly and enthusiastic individual eager to work with you.

Mike will contact you in the near future to meet you personally and discuss your needs. If you should have an immediate need for Mike's services, you may phone him at _____.

Mike and I and our whole company promise to continue our immediate and personal attention to your requirements.

Sincerely,

Alternate Wording:

(a) Mike comes to us with six years experience in our industry. He has practical knowledge of the service side of our business and has proven technical competence with all of the equipment you are now using.

Model Letter 9-6

Dear _____

You're invited to a party! We're having a get-together and **(a)** dinner next Thursday night to congratulate Chuck Wesson and give him a proper sendoff to Denver where he will be Regional Sales Manager.

I know you have enjoyed doing business with Chuck for the past three years and hate to see him go as much as I do. However, his replacement is an experienced man named Dan Briggs transferring in from our Des Moines office. Dan has been working with Chuck for the past week, and they'll have three more weeks to be sure Dan knows all of the customers and their needs before Chuck leaves. **(b)**

Dan Briggs has impressed both Chuck and me with his competence, knowledge and energy in the short time we've worked with him. His manager in Des Moines tells me his customers hated to lose Dan.

So join me and a few of Chuck's other customers next Thursday evening to meet Dan Briggs and to wish Chuck well in his new assignment.

Sincerely,

Alternate Wording:

(a) Chuck Wesson has been promoted to Regional Sales Manager of our Denver office! I know we agree that no salesman in our company could deserve the promotion more than Chuck, but you probably hate to see him go as much as I do.

(b) We are both in luck, however, because Dan Briggs who is transferring from Des Moines has a reputation for competence and service to his customers similar to Chuck's.

5. INTRODUCING THE NEW SERVICE REPRESENTATIVE

Similar to the new sales representative, introducing the new service representative requires careful groundwork. Here is a good letter of introduction.

Model Letter 9-7

Dear _____

You will be pleased to hear that John Alton, your Service Representative, has been promoted to the position of Service Manager for the Eastern Division which services the Eastern Seaboard States. His promotion has been largely due to the outstanding service he has been providing your company and others these past three years.

Ken Terry will be stepping into his shoes. It's an important responsibility that Ken will be filling and he realizes it. Keeping customers happy with their _____ equipment is an important part of our responsibility to you.

Ken comes with an excellent background. He has built an excellent base of experience as our in-house service specialist for the past two years. While there he worked directly under our Service Manager for this Division. In addition he has completed every course provided by the Company for maintaining your equipment. In short, he knows your company equipment and how to keep it running at peak efficiency.

I know you will want to welcome Ken when he calls on you next _____.

Sincerely,

6. DISCONTINUANCE OF ADVERTISING OR SALES PROMOTION SUPPORT

Dealers become attached to advertising and sales promotion support. That makes such support much more difficult to discontinue than to initiate. But circumstances do arise that make continuation of an advertising program costly and ill-advised. This letter lets the affected dealers down gently.

Model Letter 9-8

Dear _____

For the past twelve months we have been supporting our dealers in the Bismark area with regular newspaper ads promoting our _____ line. This trial effort was intended to determine if the area would respond to intensive product advertising of this type. The indication provided by you and the other Bismark dealers is that such advertising effort does not provide sufficient results to warrant continuing.

The April ad will be our last of the current type. In its place we plan to intensify our point of sale promotions. Your representative will describe the new promotion program during his next call.

Tests with other dealers similar to your situation indicate good customer interest with the new program. Sales have increased by as much as 10%. I think you will want to give it a try.

Sincerely,

7. ANNOUNCING "SPECIALS"

Any price reduction, sale or offer of extras at no increase in price deserves a general promotional effort and also offers another chance to reopen sales situations with prospects your salesmen have been unable to close.

This letter was used by the president of an automobile dealership.

Model Letter 9-9

Dear _____

I was pleased to learn that you recently visited our dealership to discuss a possible car purchase.

But I was naturally disappointed that we apparently could **(a)** not satisfy your requirements.

Each autumn we celebrate the season with our "Octoberfest Days." We have a large selection of the most popular models available at reduced prices for this annual event. I have reviewed your needs with your salesman Jerry _____, and I'm sure he can meet your requirements during this sale.

Please come to our Octoberfest and present this letter to Jerry. He will extend you every available courtesy and privilege.

Sincerely,

Alternate Wording:

(a) Although I was disappointed to hear that we could not satisfy your requirements at the time of your first visit, I'm delighted to invite you to a special event which should enable you to find exactly what you want.

8. INTRODUCING A NEW PRODUCT

When a new product is introduced, the new features and benefits must be sold, especially if the emphasis is somewhat different than past products offered. The first letter was written to automobile dealers emphasizing the advantages of more extensive available options in the new model. The second letter points out unique capabilities of a new product to users.

Model Letter 9-10

Dear _____

The success of the new _____ re-emphasizes a marketing fact. The fact is that most customers want personalized comfort and appearance items on any car they buy. The average customer is willing to pay the small additional cost for these items if he feels they will add to his overall pleasure of owning and driving his car. We sometimes become so price conscious ourselves that we forget this fact.

This year's _____ is a totally refined product by any standard—economy, reliability, time tested value. Take a close look at the optional accessory packages. Personalized luxury may be emphasized in the way one floor model or demo is equipped. Display another equipped for the enthusiast. Sportier accessory packages add that touch of pizzaz!

We've got the product! Let's display it so the buyer can see he can make his new _____ as distinctively his as he wishes.

Sincerely,

Model Letter 9-11

Dear _____

How many times have you received complaints that were the result of the dispenser and not your material?

We have developed a line of sprayers that can handle even problem materials like fish oils and wettable powders.

Don't take my word for it. Our representative, _____, will call next week to demonstrate the capabilities of this new product. We know that you will have to see it to believe it.

Sincerely,

10

TELLING YOUR CUSTOMERS YOU APPRECIATE THEIR BUSINESS

10

TELLING YOUR CUSTOMERS
YOU APPRECIATE THEIR
BUSINESS

In the rush of day to day business it is easy to forget to say "thanks." Or perhaps it seems phony or corny or inappropriate to thank customers for their business.

After all, when a sale is made the buyer benefits as much or more than the seller, doesn't he? So why should the sales organization tell the customer they appreciate the business?

Let's look at it from the buyer's point of view. Remember the real estate salesman who sold you your present home when you transferred in three or four years ago? You remember him if he sent a note (along with a "welcome" mat with your family name on it; after you moved in. You remember him if he still sends a Christmas card. And who will you list your house with if you transfer out? Or the insurance salesman or automobile salesman who thought enough of you to write a note thirty or sixty days after the sale to say "I appreciate your business and I'm here if you need me"—will they get your repeat business?

We appreciate a salesman who takes time to let us know he appreciates our business. Buyers are like that. And you can stand out from many sales organizations competing for buyers' attention just by letting them know you appreciate their business.

It is a good practice to send a carbon copy of the letter to the salesman before it is sent to his customer.

1. APPRECIATION FOR YEARS OF BUSINESS

One appropriate time to say "thanks" is on a business anniversary. Some sales managers keep a file and write appreciation letters on first, fifth, tenth or whatever anniversary of the first transaction between their company and the customer.

Model Letter 10-1

Dear _____

The other day I glanced at the first correspondence between our two companies and realized that it was five years ago that we first had the opportunity to serve you.

It made me think. I couldn't remember when I had dropped you a note just to let you know we appreciate your business.

We do appreciate your business and we look forward to serving you for the next five years.

Sincerely,

Model Letter 10-2

Dear _____

This is an anniversary of sorts and an important one for me! One year ago this month our two companies did business together for the first time.

We have enjoyed the relationship and want to thank you for the business you have placed with us. We want you to know we will continue to do our best to provide the service which justifies your faith in us. We believe we gained understanding of your particular needs during the past year which will enable us to be even more useful to you as a supplier in the next twelve months.

Sincerely,

Any holiday also provides an opportunity to express your thanks to customers. The sales manager who provided this letter decided several years ago that a personal letter at Christmas could have more sales impact with customers than a conventional card. The letter is typed on stationary with old-fashioned Christmas scene art instead of company letterhead and hand signed over the company name and sales manager's name and title.

Model Letter 10-3

Dear _____

If we ran a general store in a small town and you were a near neighbor and customer, here's what could happen:

As the Christmas season approached we would find more frequent opportunities to chat with you—we would ask if all the children would be home for Christmas—and whether you were spending the day at Aunt Kate's or if it was at your place this year.

We would also make a point of thanking you for your business during the year—"It's been a good year for us," we'd say, "but only because of loyal friends like you—and we sure do appreciate the business you give us year in and year out." We'd shake hands and a stronger bond of friendship would be cemented.

We hope that we have recaptured a little of that simple, warm, direct relationship in our dealings with you. We thank you—we enjoy working with you—and we appreciate your cordial attitude toward us. We hope you enjoy a most pleasant holiday season!

Sincerely,

2. APPRECIATION FOR A LARGE ORDER

When a buyer places an order which is unusually large or which is unusually important for him or his company, a letter from the sales manager of the sales company can be reassuring.

Model Letter 10-4

Dear _____

Thank you for the order you placed with our representative, John _____, last Thursday. We appreciate the confidence you have shown in our organization through this order.

Your order is being filled right now, and I am working with our shipping personnel to be sure everything is shipped exactly as you specified.

John _____ will call on you next Thursday to make sure everything in the shipment meets with your approval. We believe you have made a wise purchase.

Sincerely,

Model Letter 10-5

Dear _____

Thanks for taking the time to meet with our representative, Jerry _____, on a Saturday morning. He told me how important the immediate use of this program is to you and to your company.

We are now in the process of setting it up and making it happen. Jerry will be back to you with the initial plans on Wednesday and the program will be complete by *(date)* as you specified.

Again thanks, and it's great to be doing business with you.

Sincerely,

3. APPRECIATION FOR COOPERATION IN TIME OF SHORTAGE OR OTHER UNUSUAL SITUATION

Things don't always work smoothly after the sale. Raw material shortages, strikes, or unforeseen problems in production can complicate the buyer-seller relationship. When these problems occur, the salesman works hard to keep the sale glued together. When he succeeds, it is usually because he has convinced the buyer that your product is worth waiting for or that your company will come through for him in the end. Once convinced, the buyer often cooperates with sales organization rather than cancelling the order and buying from someone else.

This kind of cooperation deserves a special thanks from the sales manager. Tough letters to write, but worth it. There is a temptation to let well enough alone when your company has performed its part of the agreement, hoping the buyer will forget the difficulties involved in the sale. This sales manager chose to emphasize the positive and use the difficulties involved in the sale to cement the relationship.

Model Letter 10-6

Dear _____

I thought I heard a loud sigh of relief from your office last Friday when our shipment arrived. Even though we are over fifty miles apart I'm sure you heard my sigh of relief all the way to your building. And Jim is a new man. He was beginning to look ten years older worrying about your order—and so was I.

None of us could have anticipated the material shortage when you placed the order, but that didn't make the last few weeks any more comfortable for any of us. I want to tell you how much Jim and I appreciated your cooperation in this matter. We appreciate your believing the quality of our product was worth waiting for, and we intend to justify your faith in us and our product in the future.

Our company has learned from that experience and has taken steps which insure that this situation will not recur. I'd like to tell you about the changes we've made.

I feel that we have been "through the fire" together and would like to meet you and Jim for dinner next Tuesday to celebrate our common victory over the material shortage. Jim will pick you up at your office if that is convenient.

I look forward to meeting you Tuesday.

Sincerely,

4. APPRECIATION FOR FIRST ORDER

A conventional but important time to let customers know you appreciate their business is immediately after they place their first order.

If you let them know they are important to you at the outset, repeat orders may come sooner and easier.

Model Letter 10-7

Dear _____

Both Mr. _____, our Sales Representative, and I would like to express our sincere appreciation for the courtesies extended to us at the time of our recent visit.

We look forward to the pleasure of serving you.

If there is any way we can be of assistance, please feel free to **(a)** call on us at any time.

Sincerely,

Alternate Wording:

(a) We truly appreciate the business with which you have favored us, and look forward to the pleasure of serving you for a long time to come.

Model Letter 10-8

Dear _____

We would like to express our appreciation for the kindnesses extended to Mr. _____ on the occasion of his recent visit.

Mr. _____ indicated that you were interested in know- **(a)** ing more about our returns policy and about our Products Liability coverage.

First of all, we protect our customers' inventories by seeing to it that any merchandise which is surplus to your requirements or becomes obsolete for your equipment may be returned for full merchandise credit, providing, of course, it is in new and saleable condition.

Our Products Liability Insurance coverage is indicated by the attached Certificate of Insurance which, I am sure, is self-explanatory.

We trust that this is the information you require and, in the meantime, we would like to express our appreciation for the business with which you have favored us. We look forward to the pleasure of serving you in the future.

Sincerely,

Alternate Wording:

(a) Mr. _____ indicated that you were interested in the technical specifications of our zinc irridite plating process. I've attached information which points out the product quality and economic advantages of this process.

5. APPRECIATION FOR TESTIMONIAL FOR PRODUCT, COMPANY OR SALESMAN

When a customer provides you with a testimonial for your product, company or one of your salesmen, a warm thank you is in order. Remember, though, that you earned the praise they gave you in the testimonial. Your thank you letter must never sound as if you are thanking them for saying something your product or salesman didn't deserve.

Model Letter 10-9

Dear _____

Thank you for your kind remarks about our product in your presentation to the bankers' association last Thursday.

The experiences you related obviously came straight from your heart and I believe had a real effect on your audience. I know you are as happy to be associated with this product as a customer as I am as an employee. I had the feeling you were speaking for thousands of satisfied customers and this came through to the bankers, I'm sure.

I'm proud to represent a product that produces the results you described so well, and I'm proud to be associated with customers like you who support a product they believe in.

Thanks again.

Sincerely,

Model Letter 10-10

Dear _____

I want to thank you and everyone in your organization for choosing Dave _____ as the outstanding salesman serving _____ Hospital for 19____.

I respect Dave's professional approach to selling and am proud he is part of our organization. I particularly appreciated one paragraph in the letter you sent Dave informing him of the award:

> As you know Dave, product-oriented salesmen are easy to find, but customer-oriented ones are not. Today's hospitals need more than just commodities from salesmen; we need information too. As a customer-oriented salesman, you are aware of the total needs.

Our entire organization is proud that you have chosen Dave as the outstanding salesman serving you. All of us intend to continue to do our best to provide the quality products and services you have come to expect from Dave and our company.

Sincerely,

11

MODEL LETTERS THAT TURN CUSTOMER COMPLAINTS INTO NEW BUSINESS

11

MODEL LETTERS THAT TURN
CUSTOMER COMPLAINTS
INTO NEW BUSINESS

No one likes to receive complaints. Perhaps one reason is that we frequently do such a poor job of handling them. Either of two reactions are all too typical.

One possible reaction is to ignore the complaint. Perhaps if we ignore it, the complaint will go away. Unfortunately the customer is more likely to feel the company really doesn't care about his problem. And when he begins to doubt your desire to serve, the customer is likely to take his business to someone who does care.

The second reaction probably occurs more frequently but is just as harmful. We may feel the customer must be wrong and that the problem couldn't be as the customer describes it. So the company representative tells the customer that computers don't make mistakes—or that he just can't understand, because that's the first complaint we've ever had like that. As a result the customer feels the company doesn't want to understand or correct his problem.

The telephone is a first-line communication tool for handling complaints. It has the advantage of timeliness and provides a ready means for determining all the facts concerning the complaint. But the letter is also an important communication tool because it permits an official confirmation of the company's understanding of the customer's problem and what it intends to do to correct the situation. Proper handling of complaints requires three major steps.

1. Acknowledge the customer's point of view. The customer isn't necessarily looking for sympathy, but he is looking for someone who will understand how he feels Telling the customer that you understand takes much of the emotion out of the complaint and puts you on the side of the customer working out a solution with him.

2. Determine or review the facts involved in the complaint. If you don't know the facts that pertain to the complaint, use the telephone to get them. If this is impractical, use a letter of inquiry. A sample letter is provided on page 159. If you know the facts and are providing or confirming a solution to the customer's problem review the facts briefly. This step helps to show the customer that you understand his situation and also provides the customer with the opportunity to correct, if necessary, where you may have your facts wrong.

3. Indicate what you will do to resolve the complaint. The customer is looking for action. He doesn't care who is to blame. So resist the temptation to "pass the buck." Indicate what is to be done and when he can expect action.

The letters in this section follow this format in handling complaints.

1. RESPONDING TO A PRODUCT COMPLAINT

This letter was written to a dealer who complained that the product was not saleable in his store.

Model Letter 11-1

Dear _____

I can understand your concern with slow moving inventory as you explained in our phone conversation today. You indicated that you have sold only three cases of our product since you instituted the line six months ago—this despite promotional displays and good counter representation.   **(a)**

We will certainly cancel the balance of your order as you re-   **(b)** quest. Our sales representative will be in touch with you shortly to discuss the types of items which have the most potential in your market area. He is interested in supplying you with items which will turn over rapidly—not with putting items on your shelves which will stay there. When your inventory moves—our inventory moves!

Sincerely,

Alternate Wording:

(a)   You have prominently displayed our product and given it a fair amount of promotional effort with disappointing results.

(b)   As we discussed, several products in our line are undoubtedly better suited to your market. Our representative will call on you next week to cancel the balance of your order for this product, credit your account, and order the merchandise which has the most potential in your area.

Model Letter 11-2

Dear _____

I appreciate your bringing the problem with _____ to my attention. I can appreciate your concern with maintaining your product quality. As we discussed by telephone, here is what we know about the problem and what we will do to correct it.

You indicate the shear pin provided on the gear component is shearing at loads below that provided in the contract specifications. As a result you are receiving excessive customer complaints and service problems.

I have instructed our service engineer to call on you within   **(a)** the next two days to gather samples of the shear pins provided and to run tests on them. In addition, he is to work with your engineers to determine the adequacy of the shear load provided in the specifications with the possibility of increasing it if necessary.

Our aim is to solve the problem to your satisfaction as rapidly as possible. I will be checking with our engineer and with you after his call to confirm that you are satisfied.

Sincerely,

Alternate Wording:

(a) Our sales representative _____ will call on you within the next two days to gather samples for our engineers to test. Within a week he will return with one of our best engineers to discuss the findings and to provide any modifications necessary.

There are occasions in which the sales manager may not fully understand the nature of the complaint and finds it's impossible to telephone the customer to learn the details. This letter was written to request more information about the complaint.

Model Letter 11-3

Dear _____

I can certainly understand how you must feel concerning your experience using our paint on your home. Considerable labor goes into painting a home, not to mention the cost of the paint used. To have it peel in one year creates undue frustration. Before I can assist you in resolving the problem you describe, I will need some additional facts. If you will provide them, we will do our utmost to provide a satisfactory solution.

Here's what I need to know:

1. What type of surface was our product applied on?
2. What time of the year was it applied?
3. What type of paint was used previously?
4. How did you prepare the paint and the surface for application?

Thank you for your help. We value you as a customer and want to do everything we can to keep you returning to _____ as the answer to your painting needs.

Sincerely,

2. RESPONDING TO A SERVICE COMPLAINT

Service is often an important ingredient to a company's success and its quality must be vigorously maintained. Complaints are frequently encountered here since service largely involves the human factor.

This letter was written to an irate consumer who was dissatisfied with the appliance service she had received.

Model Letter 11-4

Dear _____

I am terribly sorry to learn of your problems with _____. I understand how you must feel. The problem has not only been an inconvience and cost to you, but also must have been a frustration as you sought to have the problem corrected.

As I understand your problem, you have had three timers installed in your _____ in the past twelve months and all have failed. The first time the dealer replaced the timer without charge for the timer or labor. The second time he provided the timer without charge but charged for labor. The third time he charged you for time and labor. You feel the repairs should have been made without cost because you believe there must be some inherent fault in the product to cause the timers to fail in this manner.

It is our sincere desire to make sure each and every customer is completely satisfied with her purchase. And although our dealer acted in accordance with the terms of our warranty, we will be happy to reimburse you for the cost of the timer and two service calls. If you will forward your receipts for the calls, we will promptly reimburse you.

In the meantime we are having a company serviceman call on you to completely check out your machine and to locate any cause for the repeated failure of the timers on your _____. I'm sorry this problem has occurred, but I am pleased that we have had the opportunity to correct it and to help you join the many thousands of satisfied _____ customers.

Sincerely,

3. RESPONDING TO A COMPLAINT CONCERNING A SALESMAN

People problems are perhaps the most difficult to resolve. Poor communications, poor human relations, and just plain personality conflicts sometimes create friction that must be properly handled. Frequently the solution to such problems is difficult. A personality conflict might be resolved by switching the account to another salesman. But what if the account is not conveniently located for the attention of another salesman? Communication and human relations problems can sometimes be resolved with proper training, but the process is often slow and complex.

When a complaint occurs involving your salesman, prompt and personal attention is demanded. The telephone is often the best way to get a full understanding of the problem. The letter is an appropriate means for follow-up and providing a sure understanding of what is agreed to as a solution.

Model Letter 11-5

Dear _____

Thank you for calling me today concerning the problem you are having with _____. I am happy you have the confidence in us to bring the problem to our attention. I can certainly understand how you must feel in such a situation.

I have discussed the problem with _____ and have his agreement as to the remedy we discussed. As a result _____ will be calling on you within the next few days as your Sales Representative. I think you will like _____. He is personable and eager to serve. He has been calling on customers with needs similar to yours and understands them well.

Again, thank you for bringing the problem to our attention.

Sincerely,

Model Letter 11-6

Dear _____

After our conversation the other day I can understand why you feel the way you do about our sales representative, Bill Smith. I appreciate you phoning me about the incident rather than discontinuing business with us.

However, I do feel personally responsible for the incident. We certainly don't train our salesmen to argue with customers and insult them. I have not been coaching Bill regularly as I should, and his behavior the other day is really due to my not doing my job. As I mentioned to you on the phone, Bill knows our product inside out. He can analyze a customer's installation and spot opportunities to cut costs and increase production faster than any man in the industry. He could be a great asset to his customers if he could learn to listen to them and understand wht their objectives are so that he can be of help to them. But he tends to tell the customer what to do on the basis of the best engineering method rather than finding out if that method really makes sense in the customer's operation. **(a)**

Today I talked to Bill about this tendency. He sees it as a **(b)** problem and is willing to work to improve. He realizes his know-it-all attitude has kept him from being of real value to customers in the past. He and I have agreed upon a coaching schedule to enable him to put his technical knowledge to work for his customers.

When he calls on you next month I believe you'll find him a changed man. I appreciate your cooperation very much.

Sincerely,

Alternate Wording:

(a) As we agreed on the phone, Bill is undoubtedly one of the most knowledgeable men in our industry from an engineering standpoint. However, he does not listen to the customer to determine the customer's exact requirements. I owe it to Bill and especially to his customers to develop this ability in him so that his technical expertise can be applied to the customer's requirements.

(b) Today I talked to Bill about the need to listen to his customers and he was very receptive. It seems he has been close to arguments with customers several times. He finds this very frustrating, because he really is sincerely trying to help his customers cut costs and increase productivity.

4. RESPONDING TO A PRICE COMPLAINT

Pricing is a frequent source for complaints. Three types are likely. The customer may complain that he has paid more for your product than he would have paid for a competitor's product. Or he may complain about an alleged pricing or extension error. Or you may receive complaints from dealers who feel that insufficient margin is available to profitably handle your product. A model letter is provided for each of these needs.

Model Letter 11-7

Dear _____

Thank you for letting us know about your concern that you were overcharged for the sofa you purchased from us last week. In this day of inflationary pressures each of us must endeavor to get the greatest value from every investment.

As I understand your letter, you feel you could have gotten essentially the same quality sofa from _____ for about $50 less than you paid for the _____ you purchased from us. As a result, you would like to either return the sofa or receive a refund in that amount from us.

First, let me assure you we will do everything possible to make you happy with your purchase. We value you for your repeated purchases and because we know you will tell your friends and neighbors when you are happy.

Comparing furniture is a troublesome task as I am sure you know from considering your decision to purchase from _____. Many qualities may be built into the item that are not readily evident but may lend considerably to the expected life and enjoyment of the product. Fabric, spring construction and frame construction are just three.

May I suggest this as a possible solution. Within the next few days come down to the store and ask for me. I will be happy to describe to you the features that are built into the _____ line that will provide many more years of expected life than any other line. Then if you still feel the other brand provides the best value, we will be happy to return the sofa for a full refund.

Fair enough? I will be looking for you at the store one day soon.

Sincerely,

This letter was written for the pricing complaint that was due to hat the customer felt was improper extension of an invoice.

Model Letter 11-8

Dear _____

I'm happy you indicated your concern for the price that was charged for the _____ on invoice _____. Each of us is willing to pay the worth of a product but no more.

We believe the billing extension is correct. The current price is _____ as was announced in a price adjustment letter on October 1. The extension for the number ordered is also correct.

We certainly do make billing errors from time to time despite our care to make sure each invoice is correct in every detail. And it keeps us on our toes to know that our customers are watching us as we go. Thanks!

Sincerely,

The following model letter was written in response to a dealer who complained that insufficient margin was provided on a product to make handling it profitable.

Model Letter 11-9

Dear _____

J can certainly understand your desire to secure a fair margin on every product you handle. We strive for the same end result.

As we discussed by telephone, our products are generally priced to permit you to enjoy a 30% mark-up since it has been provided mainly as a price competitive product. As you are aware, competitors have been making the customer keenly aware of price for the past year. And although we don't agree with their marketing practices, we must compete. As a result we developed the product in question. We have cut our margin on this product to the bone. And we felt our dealers would want to do the same so you could meet competitive offers. As a result your expected margin on the economy model is only 15%.

The value in the economy line is not in the sales you make of that item, but in the opportunity it provides for trading up to the better lines once the customer enters your store.

I hope this explanation answers your question concerning our price structure. You are an important dealer and we want to maintain your confidence.

Sincerely,

12

LETTERS THAT OPEN THE DOOR FOR THE SALESMAN'S CALL

LETTERS THAT OPEN
THE DOOR FOR THE
SALESMAN'S CALL

The salesman can't sell until he has the opportunity to meet his prospect face-to-face. But getting the initial appointment sometimes represents as much of a sales job as that which must occur during the appointment.

With only so much time available to invest, the prospect must allocate it where he feels he will most benefit. So your efforst to secure a first appointment must show the prospect how he stands to benefit from investing his time with you.

The telephone and the letter each have their place when making appointments. The telephone is valuable because of its immediacy. And it provides for more accurate determination of the prospect's initial reaction to your request. The letter avoids the problem of reaching the prospect at an inopportune time. It affords the opportunity for presenting credentials. And it can often be combined with the follow-up telephone call to make a very effective appointment making combination.

A letter seeking an appointment is a miniature sales call. As such it involves three elements. First, it must provide some potential benefit to the prospect for granting the interview you request. Second, it must briefly review the facts that will assist the prospect to make an evaluation of what you ask. And third, it should hold forth the next step—the action you seek. In many instances, the next step sought by the letter is a follow-up telephone call for an appointment.

Many of the letters in this chapter could be sent by the sales manager or could be used by your salesmen. You might also consider going through the letters in this chapter and selecting those you believe your salesmen could use most effectively. You could make any minor revisions necessary to tailor them to your market and then hold a sales meeting with your salesmen. In your sales meeting you could provide the selected letters to your salesmen and also discuss with them how to use the letters most effectively as part of their total sales approach.

1. SEEKING APPOINTMENT WITH NO PREVIOUS CONTACTS

Perhaps the most difficult appointment to secure is where no previous contact has been made with the prospect and where no mutual acquaintance or interest is available to serve as an opener. So let's tackle that one first. This letter could be sent by the sales manager or by the salesman. It sets up a telephone call to follow shortly behind the letter.

Model Letter 12-1

Dear _____

If you are like most busy executives, you can always squeeze in time to keep abreast of the latest developments and ideas in diode engineering.

My schedule brings me to your city on ____*(date)*____ . I **(a)** would appreciate an opportunity to meet with you at your convenience to share some ideas which may be useful to you.

I shall telephone you in a few days to make an appointment. **(b)**

Sincerely,

Alternate Wording:

(a) I believe I have some new ideas to share which may be useful to you.

(b) I will arrive in your city Monday and will count on meeting with you for lunch if that is convenient for you. I'll telephone you Thursday to confirm our meeting.

Here is another letter designed to accomplish the same purpose. This one is longer, but is just as powerful.

Model Letter 12-2

Dear _____

Enclosed are our company brochure and other printed materials which will give you details on the scope, dimension and professionalism of the _____ organization.

We believe you will agree that communication is one of the vital keys to modern marketing in today's highly competitive business society. Executives spend sleepless nights mulling over people problems because it takes emotional and unpredictable people to produce and sell products and services to equally emotional and unpredictable customers.

The problems of communicating are tremendous, and yet we are in an age of technological explosion wherein the changes portending in the next ten years stagger the imagination. Our services can help you *solve your communication problem—*both external and internal.

We are staffed and geared to take on an entire assignment—   **(a)**
analysis, planning, creating, staging—with printed materials, incentive programs, motion pictures, slides, filmstrips, multimedia shows, exhibits—everything you need to schieve your objectives.

Recent projects include *(select some recent programs that would be of interest to the prospect.)*

May I have an opportunity to meet with you and show you examples of our work? Unless I hear from you sooner, I plan to contact you in a few days to set up an appointment.

Sincerely,

Alternate Wording:

(a) Our list of satisfied clients reads like *Fortune's* list of top ranking U.S. corporations but also includes many smaller companies interested in growing and increasing profits. Our motion picture productions have won over 150 awards for excellence from film festivals all over the world. Our three convenient studio locations mean your job can be done where it should be done with dispatch and economy.

This letter provides a novel approach.

Model Letter 12-3

Dear _____

Are you besieged with solicitations about premium ideas and new ideas to save and make you money? Where do most of them end up—in your waste basket?

Stop! Don't throw this letter away! Reading the next paragraph could improve your company's profit.

We are professional problem solvers. The enclosed Fact Sheet describes just one problem we solved for   *(name of a customer)*

We would like to include _____ as one of our satisfied clients. When can we get together and tap our know-how and experience in your behalf? Increased sales and profits become mutual goals when we join forces.

We'll come to you. No obligation. Just say when!

Sincerely,

The above letter is one of a series that is sent to a prospect. Here is another in the series. When two or three letters of this type have been sent to the prospect, the salesman calls for an appointment.

Model Letter 12-4

Dear _____

Does the name ___*(name of your company)*___ ring a bell? We solve problems!

The enclosed fact sheet reveals another marketing problem solved for   *(name of client)*

What is your biggest hang-up? We want to put our collective brains to work on it—why not challenge us? We guarantee results.

Just pick up your phone and dial _____—you'll get attention.

Sincerely,

2. SEEKING APPOINTMENT BASED ON A REFERRAL

A referral provides a solid basis for securing a first call appointment. Customers, friends, suppliers all provide a mutual point of reference to get receptivity. In addition, references provide a low key sense of obligation—not an obligation to buy, surely, but at least an obligation to provide you the courtesy of attention.

Model Letter 12-5

Dear _____

Interested in reducing your packaging costs by as much as 10%? That's what Bill Johnson at Acme Manufacturing was able to accomplish.

As a direct result of his excellent savings achievement, he **(a)** feels he would like to share the same possiblity with some of his friends. So he happily consented to my writing this letter.

I will be in the Chicago area on Tuesday, February 6. I would **(b)** be happy to explain in detail how Bill was able to achieve such significant cost reductions. Interested? I'll call you this week to set an appointment.

Sincerely,

Alternate Wording:

(a) Bill believes the simple, common sense approach we take to packaging may be interesting to you and was happy to allow me to mention his satisfaction to you.

(b) I believe you will be interested in how such cost reductions can be achieved. I will phone you this week to set an appointment for Tuesday, February 6 or Wednesday, February 7.

This letter was written by a retail furniture sales manager as a result of a lead from one of his customers.

Model Letter 12-6

Dear _____

When you locate a store that really cares about you and goes out of its way to make you a satisfied customer, you want to tell the world. And that's just what is happening with Mrs. Jane Meyers. She has been so pleased with her recent purchases at _____ that she wants you to know.

Mrs. Meyers' experience is not at all unusual. As a matter of fact we usually succeed in getting that type of enthusiastic endorsement from our customers.

Give us a try. You, too, may want to do a little shouting about your satisfaction with _____.

Sincerely,

3. LETTERS OF REPLY TO UNSOLICITED REQUESTS FOR INFORMATION

Depending on the type of product or service you sell, prospects may come to you seeking information about your product. The customer is most likely to take the initiative in response to advertising or conversations with customers. Occasionally, prospects may write to inquire if you can fill a particular need. This type of unique sales opportunity calls for a well-written sales letter. Here are several.

Model Letter 12-7

Here is the _____ literature you requested. We have **(a)** tried to make the information provided there as complete as possible. But we have not been able to tailor the application of the product to your specific situation. Only a personal meeting can do that.

When you have had a chance to read the literature and to **(b)** determine if the _____ line seems to fit your needs, I will have our salesman, Mr. _____ call you for an appointment. In that way he will be able to provide you with the information you need to determine *exactly* what you might expect in the way of performance and precisely which model will best fit your needs.

I'll have him call you on Thursday.

Sincerely,

Alternate Wording:

(a) Thank you for your request for additional information and literature. I was not completely sure which model and what optional equipment would fit your needs and did not wish to send information which did not apply.

(b) I have asked our representative Mr. _____ to call on you so that you may determine exactly what you might expect in the way of performance and precisely which model will best fit your needs.

Perhaps you use your advertising program as a source of sales leads. Many companies use a coupon in their ads to solicit inquiries. In addition, some prospects may write letters of inquiry concerning some ad they have seen. This letter was written replying to such an inquiry.

Model Letter 12-8

Dear _____

We are pleased that you have asked for particulars concerning our _____ line as advertised in the December issue of _____. Additional information is enclosed.

We have been featuring the _____ line for the past several months in the _____ Journal because of its unique application to your type of business. In fact we now have over 140 customers using the _____ line in applications similar to yours.

Since you may have questions remaining even after you have read the enclosed literature, I have asked our Representative, _____, to call you some time in the next few days.

Thanks for your interest in the _____.

Sincerely,

This letter was written in response to a prospect who wrote to the company inquiring if the company had a product that could fill a particular need.

Model Letter 12-9

Dear _____

Thank you for thinking of _____ to fill your needs. We manufacture 32 different models of valves that might fit the application you describe. So surely at least one of them will meet your needs precisely.

I have asked our sales representative, _____, to call you in the next few days. With a better idea of your application, he will be able to recommend the particular valve to meet your requirements.

We appreciate the opportunity to be of service and look forward to assisting you further.

Sincerely,

4. LETTER TO TRADE SHOW REGISTRANTS

Another valuable source for prospect leads may be trade shows, fairs, etc., which provide the opportunity to display your products to potential buyers. Many marketers offer registration opportunities at their display booths in return for prizes or other incentives. The prospect registration provides an expanded mailing list that should be quickly followed up with a letter and a salesman visit if warranted.

Here is a letter that provides a good follow-up to a trade show registration.

Model Letter 12-10

Dear _____

Thank you for visiting our booth at the Housewares Show. As you saw, we have many products that offer outstanding merchanidising and profit opportunities. For example, you may have seen ___*(two or three products)*___ —just to name a few.

Enclosed are wholesale prices and catalog pages for the com- **(a)**
ing product season. In addition, we provide an attractive discount program and frequent incentives.

Our products will be supported by an intensive advertising
program right in your local area.

We would like to consider you as a proud dealer of
_____ products. Our Sales Representative will be in-
contact with you in the next week or two to answer any questions you might have.

Sincerely,

Alternate Wording:

(a) We hope these products interested you. We would like the
opportunity to discuss some additional advantages of our
product such as an attractive discount program and intensive
advertising.

5. "THANK YOU" FOR COURTESIES SHOWN OUR SALESMAN

Follow-up after the salesman's first call is important for two
reasons. A follow-up letter provides the opportunity to put your company's name before the prospect one more time to better fix its image
in his mind. In addition, a follow-up letter provides a necessary
demonstration of appreciation for the prospect's hospitality. The
following letters provide a sound basis for follow-up.

Model Letter 12-11

Dear _____

I enjoyed our meeting yesterday and I appreciate it.

As you review our proposal, I hope you will consider carefully two very important benefits your company will enjoy:

    1.   You will be able to reduce your payroll preparation
        costs by as much as $8,500 per year;

    2.   You will be able to quickly receive the cost analysis
        reports you require to control your business effec-
        tively. These reports will be provided with no time

Enclosed is the booklet I promised. Notice on Page 3 the ex- **(a)**
perience related by one of our customers. You will find the

comments are rather typical of the results to be expected from our automated payroll service.

I will call you later this week to discuss your reaction to the program.

Sincerely,

Alternate Wording:

(a) Enclosed is the booklet I promised. I have also attached the names of several customers whose circumstances are similar to yours. These companies have received the benefits which we discussed. You may be interested in talking to them.

Model Letter 12-12

Dear _____

Thank you for the opportunity to meet with you at your office. The time you took from your busy schedule to spend with me was both enjoyable and rewarding. I trust it was rewarding to you as well. Your thoughts provided me a much clearer picture of your firm's operations.

Please give some thought to the various services we discussed **(a)** and we'll be looking forward to the possiblity of working with you on any special projects you may be planning within our area of specialty.

I shall make it a point to keep in touch and hope you will not hesitate to call us should you desire further information or assistance on a specific project.

Sincerely,

Alternate Wording:

(a) I believe several of the services we discussed may be helpful to you in the near future.

13

**TESTED LETTERS THAT
HELP SALESMEN AND
SALES MANAGERS COLLECT
DELINQUENT ACCOUNTS**

13

TESTED LETTERS THAT
HELP SALESMEN AND SALES
MANAGERS COLLECT
DELINQUENT ACCOUNTS

If delinquent accounts are ignored, they will become more difficult to collect without losing a customer.

Some sales organizations expect the sales manager to be responsible for collecting delinquent accounts in the early stages, but transfer the responsibility for collection to the credit department at some agreed upon point, for instance sixty or ninety days past due. Other companies are not so departmentalized, and the sales department is totally responsible for collections. Still other companies are rigidly departmentalized and the sales manager would rarely be involved in prompting payment from accounts. No matter which approach your company follows, some of the letters in this chapter will be valuable to you.

A large part of your job is to keep your salesmen selling at peak efficiency, and one part of that job is to structure your salesmen's function to emphasize productive direct-selling activities. Some non-sales activities must be tolerated as a necessary evil in most sales jobs; however, non-sales producing activities should be minimized. One responsibility which may be included in the sales job is the collection of overdue accounts.

For most salesmen this is a difficult and distasteful task. A salesman can spend an inordinate amount of time and effort worrying about stimulating slow paying accounts and, as a result, his sales production may suffer. Use of these letters can avoid that consequence.

The salesman should know about all correspondence with his customer, ideally before it is sent to the customer. In some sales organizations this requires coordination with the credit department. In some cases, letters stimulating payment from overdue accounts originate from the line sales manager. In these cases, the salesman should receive a copy of the correspondence before it is sent to the customer and the letter should smooth the way for the salesman.

1. DECLINING A REQUEST FOR SPECIAL TERMS

Occasionally a customer will ask the salesman for preferential credit terms which the salesman does not have the authority to grant. The salesman will then bring the request to the sales manager. Particularly if a large account is involved, the salesman may make a strong pitch for granting the customer's request. The sales manager may consider the request himself or, if necessary, take it up with the appropriate authority in the company. When the decision is against granting the requested special terms, the sales manager has to reply to the customer in a way that does not alienate him.

Model Letter 13-1

Dear _____

Bill brought your request for cash discount terms to me and he and I have explored the possibility with the appropriate people in our company. Bill and I received a short college course in pricing from our credit and accounting people in the process, by the way.

As you know, our products are priced as low as anyone in the (a) industry. From our accounting department's standpoint the credit terms offered to the market are as much a cost of the product as assembly or machining or any other production cost. Their answer to me was that any cost savings they can make in the future will be passed on to the customer. But right now the price of our product is as low as possible without sacrificing the quality you must have.

So, for the present, I must tell you that it is not possible to offer cash discount terms.

Bill will be in to see you next week to discuss an innovative product which may help lower your costs and will be glad to answer any other questions you have at that time.

Sincerely,

Alternate Wording:

(a)   Without "passing the buck" to our credit department. let me pass on the explanation they gave me. Since cash discount terms are a discount for prompt payment, those terms are usually taken into consideration when products are priced. Our company's policy has been to price our products as low as possible to begin with. So, from our accounting department's point of view, the cash discount is being given to our customers in advance.

2.   PROMPTING AN ACCOUNT AT FIRST SIGN OF SLOWNESS IN PAYMENT

You may have a set policy to follow when an account does not pay within the agreed terms. Generally, a friendly reminder when the account first goes past the agreed terms is productive in several ways. It serves as a "temperature take" to find out if you have a collection problem. The invoice may simply have been misplaced and the friendly reminder brings it to the account's attention and brings payment with no loss of goodwill. The customer may have some questions about the bill and the reminder will prompt him to call and get the answers. The account may not have been satisfied with his order and the letter will prompt him to air his grievance so the salesman can deal with it. This letter should be simply a reminder, and it should assume that the customer is satisfied, intended to pay within the agreed terms, but may have simply overlooked or misplaced the invoice.

Model Letter 13-2

Dear _____

The last few days have been hectic. When I cleaned out my **(a)** "In" box this morning I found several invoices from suppliers dangerously close to past due.

I suspect you've been in a similar situation recently and our invoice _____ dated _____ is on the bottom of your "In" basket, on your secretary's desk, or lost in the accounting department.

Just put it through for payment, or when Bob calls on you next week tell him to bill you again if the original invoice hasn't turned up.

Sincerely,

Alternate Wording:

(a) Several invoices were already past the due date. Next I looked over the invoices sent to our customers sixty days ago and noticed one sent to you.

Model Letter 13-3

Dear _____

I was reviewing last month's shipments this morning and, seeing several orders from you, was reminded again of the ideal working relationship we have. I appreciate the business we receive from you and wanted to remind you that I am here if I can be of service in any way.

I know your sales have been increasing and it is good to see you having such a great year. Would you take a minute to check on a couple of invoices for me? My records show invoices _____ and _____ unpaid from last month. Just send them through for payment when they appear, or let

Bob know if there is any problem with them when he calls on you next week.

Thanks again,

3. PROMPTING AN ACCOUNT A SECOND TIME WHEN SLOWNESS PERSISTS

When you have brought past due invoices to the buyer's attention with a friendly reminder and receive no response, it is time for a more direct approach. Your company may have a set policy for dealing with these situations. You may wish to send a carbon copy of this letter to your internal credit department or credit manager. The account is probably approximately sixty days past due at this point, and the policy of some companies would dictate turning correspondence over to the credit department at this point.

Model Letter 13-4

Dear _____

I wrote you last month regarding these invoices:

Date	Number	Amount

Tom will be calling on you next week. He will be prepared to **(a)** answer any questions you have. I have instructed him to bring back a check and give you a receipt clearing up these old invoices.

Sincerely,

Alternate Wording:

(a) I will phone you Friday morning to discuss these invoices prior to Tom's visit.

Model Letter 13-5

Dear _____

We discussed invoices _____ and _____ last month and determined that they were accurate. It was my understanding that you would send payment shortly. Phil will be calling on you next Wednesday. Perhaps the most practical way to clear these invoices would be to pull them out of the normal accounting routine and hand Phil a check when he comes in Wednesday. **(a)**

I'll be talking to him by phone on Friday, and I'll remind him to ask you for a check and give you a paid receipt when he visits you.

Sincerely,

Alternate Wording:

(a) I know invoices can get lost in the shuffle of daily bookkeeping. So, may I suggest you pull these invoices out of your normal accounting routine and hand Phil a check this Wednesday.

4. INFORMING A CUSTOMER THAT YOUR INTERNAL CREDIT DEPARTMENT WILL BE CONTACTING HIM

Some companies have a policy of turning correspondence over to the credit department when the sales department has not been able to prompt payment within a certain time (usually sixty to ninety days). Informing the customer that the credit department is taking over can give the sales manager one more chance to collect amicably.

Model Letter 13-6

Dear _____

We have discussed your outstanding balance several times in the last two months. I believe we agree that our product is most suitable to your production methods and we wish to continue as your supplier.

The amount and age of your outstanding invoices force me to turn over correspondence on this matter to our credit manager at the end of this month unless payment is received before that date.

I will phone you this Friday to discuss payment. I want to continue to serve you on open account, and I believe you see advantages to your company in continuing to deal with us on open account.

Let's clear this matter up on Friday.

Sincerely,

5. INFORMING AN ACCOUNT YOU MUST SELL ON A CASH BASIS

Occasionally your credit department will accept orders on a cash basis only from a particular account. If you make your own credit decisions, you may also come to the conclusion that a particular account should be sold on a cash basis because of past paying record, weak financial condition, or other valid reasons.

Although this is a difficult letter to write, it need not sound cold and legalistic. This letter was written by a sales manager who could not extend open-account terms, but wanted the business enough to sell the customer on the advantages of buying on a cash basis.

Model Letter 13-7

Dear _____

I want to thank you for your order of January 15th. The advantage of our plating method goes further than just lower initial cost. The superior durability will be an attractive plus to your customers and will give your salesmen the edge in a competitive market.

We will ship your order on a cash basis and of course you will receive our cash discount further lowering your cost.

We value your business and hope that you agree with the cost and quality advantages of this arrangement.

Sincerely,

6. INFORMING A CUSTOMER THAT THE ACCOUNT IS BEING TURNED OVER TO COLLECTORS

Occasionally you will have to sigh, "Can't win 'em all" and turn an account over to an outside collector. When you reach this point, you will already have been through the steps of gently reminding, less subtle and firmer reminders which aim to keep the account as an active customer as well as prompt payment. You are to the point of not wanting future business from the account—you just want your money.

Model Letter 13-8

Gentlemen:

It seldom becomes necessary for us to turn an account over to an attorney for collection. And on those few occasions when circumstances leave us no alternative, we consider it only fair to tell the customer exactly what we intend to do.

Certainly you realize that we have made every effort to be **(a)** fair and patient in requesting you to settle your account of $_____.

We have written to you several times, asking that you let us know how we could cooperate with you in getting the indebtedness straightened out.

Your continued silence leaves us no alternative but reluctant- **(b)** ly to refer your account to our attorney for collection. So, won't you respond to this final appeal for your cooperation and avoid a procedure that can only mean additional expense to you?

Unless we hear from you within five days we shall be compelled to transfer your account to the office of our attorney.

Very truly yours,

Alternate Wording:

(a) We have been most patient in awaiting payment of your long past due obligation. However, despite our sincere spirit of cooperation, we have had no word or check from you in answer to our request.

(b) We must now insist that payment be forwarded at once. If we do not receive your check in ten days, your account will be turned over to our attorney.

Model Letter 13-9

Gentlemen:

Again, we ask you to respond regarding the following invoices:

Date	Reference	Amount

You have chosen to ignore our previous requests for **(a)** payment of these long past due invoices. Do not force us to take more direct action to collect this amount.

If we do not receive payment within ten days, our attorney **(b)** will become responsible for collecting the amount due.

Very truly yours,

Alternate Wording:

(a) We have written you on numerous occasions regarding your past due account but you continue to ignore your obligation.

(b) Your failure to comply to our justified requests for payment has forced us to turn your account over to _____ Collection Service. A representative of their firm will contact you at the expiration of the additional ten day grace period we have allowed you.

We strongly urge you to take advantage of this grace period to avoid costly litigation expenses.

7. ENCOURAGING CUSTOMERS TO TAKE DISCOUNTS

There are times when prompt payment from suppliers may be important to you, or you may have customers who you believe would increase their purchases if they lowered their per unit cost by availing themselves of your most attractive discount terms.

Model Letter 13-10

Dear _____

Thank you for the order you placed January 16. I noted that this was the second order you have placed for this new type bushing and asked Tom about it. He told me how you have found a way to simplify an assembly operation and thereby reduce labor cost by using this bushing. I'm glad we can help as you continue to find ways to reduce costs while increasing quality in a competitive industry.

I know this is important to you and believe I can suggest a way to reduce costs even further. We offer 1/10/Net 30 terms and you have always been extremely prompt in paying invoices—thirty days or less. I suspect you could have payment sent in 10 days just as easily and take the 1% discount. Our company recently checked our own accounts payable accounting methods and found we were missing discount terms by just a few days in many cases.

Tom will check with you on his next call to see if this is practical with your accounting methods. We want to assist you in maintaining quality and reducing costs in every way we can.

Sincerely,

Model Letter 13-11

Dear _____

Would you be interested in increasing your profit margin on our products at retail by 2%? We are proud of the substantial margin our dealers earn on our products, but in looking over the orders you have placed over the past six months, I believe there is an opportunity for you to further increase your profit on our merchandise.

We offer 2/10/Net 30 terms, a real opportunity for additional profits which is easily overlooked. Try it on your next order—I think you'll like that extra 2%.

Sincerely,

8. USING CREDIT MESSAGES TO INVITE ADDITIONAL PURCHASES FROM YOUR BEST CUSTOMERS

Whether you deal with consumers, retailers, wholesalers or industrial customers, you can use credit messages to invite additional purchases from your best customers. You may want to use special V.I.P. identification cards or numbers. You may wish to have your credit manager send out your message rather than have it come from the sales department. You may wish to use mailgrams to add weight to your message. Whatever devices you use the message should clearly say, "You're a very important customer. Your credit is good with us. We want to be sure you get extra special treatment."

Model Letter 13-12

Dear _____

The purpose of this letter is to confirm the excellent status of your credit account.

Because our credit department appreciates the splendid manner in which you have done business with us in the past, we consider it a privilege to issue you the special V.I.P. card enclosed. Use this card or the V.I.P. number and it will identify you to all of our credit, sales, and service personnel as a very special person. It is a pleasure to do business with you.

Sincerely,

14

MODEL INVITATIONS
TO SPECIAL EVENTS THAT
GET CUSTOMER ACTION

14

MODEL INVITATIONS
TO SPECIAL EVENTS THAT
GET CUSTOMER ACTION

Not every request a sales department makes of a customer or prospect is a request to buy. Sometimes what you seek is a commitment of the body—to get the prospect or customer to agree to attend some function you are holding.

For example, you may be seeking his attendance at a trade show or at a special company meeting. Perhaps it's to visit your office or plant. Whatever the reason, a sale is involved just as when you are selling a product or service. The customer may not be putting out cold hard cash, but he is investing his time. And for some that's even more precious.

The letter is a valuable tool for getting the customer's commitment to act on your invitation. It can be personal, can have the advantage of remaining on his desk for lingering attention and can often be combined with the personal call, either by telephone or in person, to spur him to action.

Just one caution, though. When you use a letter without a planned personal follow-up, provide some method for the customer to respond to your letter of invitation. Seek some immediate action on his part, be it the return of a postcard or a telephone call. If you don't, the importance of the action you seek is likely to recede as time passes until he forgets all about it by the time you want him to act.

1.   LETTERS OF INVITATION TO VISIT TRADE SHOW

The trade show is a time-established method for introducing new models, for informing buyers of new marketing trends, and for attracting new customers and dealers. It is an important and busy time of the year for many marketing organizations.

Although the trade show may attract many potential dealers and buyers, there is no assurance they will visit your booth. Competition for the visitor's attention is normally keen. Every participating company seeks a method for focusing attention on its display.

One effective means to secure a competitive edge is to command advance interest in your booth by means of advertising and letter. A letter to your customers and prospects alerts them that they will find an answer to their needs at your booth. Hopefully the prospect will seek you out. At the very least, it should help him recognize your company name when he spots it among the myriad of displays at the trade show.

Model Letter 14-1

Dear _____

Visit The _____ *Trade Show!!*

Why? It's the one big opportunity that all distributors have for examining new lines, becoming familiar with suppliers, keeping in touch with what's happening in our ever-changing business.

If you're considering broadening your line, be sure to check us out. You'll find our display of 47 _____*(type of product)*_____ items at _____*(booth location)*_____.

We have some top potential areas open, and we're looking for the best distributors in the business to fill them. If you qualify, you will be joining a growing organization that offers a top quality product supported with excellent advertising, sales promotion and sales help.

Look us up at the trade show. We'll be happy to take the time to prove to you that a move to _____ can be your best marketing decision all year.

Sincerely,

Model Letter 14-2

_____ _____ _____   **Invitation—**
                                           Front Cover
invites you to

A MANAGEMENT PREVIEW   **Invitation—**
OF   **Inside Back Cover**
NEWEST MARKING AND
LABELING SYSTEMS

Time to re-evaluate your labeling and marking?
Please join us at 1:30 p.m.

. . . then hear

_____ _____ Specialists

- - - - - - - - - - Outline - - - - - - - - - -

The newest techniques and ideas for getting the most from your marking and labeling systems. Learn how others are using our systems to get more done at less cost in over 50,000 companies.

- -

DATE: April 23, 19___

TIME: 1:30 p.m. only

PLACE: Holiday Inn Room C
                           Exit 12 - Marine Turnpike
                           Auburn, ME 04210

            R.S.V.P.   Light Refreshments

_____ _____ _____

- -

TRAVELING TRADE SHOW   Response
                                            Card

☐ Will Attend   ☐ Will Not Attend

Holiday Inn—Room C
Exit 12-Marine Turnpike
Auburn, ME 04210

Name	Title
Name	Title
Company	
Address	

Model Letter 14-3

Dear _____

Industry experts are predicting that more than   *(number of units)*   of the rapidly growing   *(name of line)*   will be sold in the coming year. That's a sizeable market. If you're considering getting in on the action but haven't yet decided on the best company and brand to go with, be sure to stop by our display at the _____ Show at McCormick Place next month.

You'll find 21 models on display, the most extensive in the industry. You'll also find a complete display of our advertising and sales promotion programs. A knowledgeable   *(name of company)*   representative will be on hand to explain our dealer program and to answer your questions.

You might want to visit our booth first. That way you'll have a good comparison to use as you take in the other displays at the show.

Bring this letter along and present it to one of the men at our **(a)** display. It will help to identify you as a special visitor. And for that we will be happy to give you a copy of the book "_____" just as our way of saying thanks for stopping by.

Sincerely,

Alternate Wording:

(a) Just in hope of getting to know you better, we are holding a hospitality hour each evening of the trade show Drop by, won't you, any evening from 7 thru 10:30 p.m. Just bring this letter and we'll be most happy to introduce you around.

(a) Many of those planning to attend the show have indicated a desire to see some of our models in operation. So we have planned a special demonstration each day of the trade show. Simply ask for details at our display.

2. FOLLOW-UP TO A TRADE SHOW

Your trade show exhibit may have developed a slender thread of interest in the prospects who visited—a thread that is easily broken in the days that follow. To enjoy maximum benefit from your trade show investment of time and money, it's crucial that you provide some method for registering all visitors and initiating a follow-up contact with them immediately after the show. One proven successful technique is to send a thank-you letter quickly upon completion of the show and then have a salesman contact the prospect shortly after that.

Model Letter 14-4

Dear _____

Thank you for visiting our booth at the Housewares Show. As you saw, we have many products that offer outstanding merchandising and profit opportunities. Some of our new products such as _____, offer exciting growth potential. Others have long been established in the market and have built the name of _____ as one of quality in the minds of the customer.

I hope you had the opportunity to see something of our advertising plans for the year when you visited our booth. They're exciting and offer great sales opportunities right in your own marketing area.

Enclosed are wholesale prices and catalog pages for the _____. In addition there is a 5% advertising allowance and if your order is received before the deadlines shown on the attached sales program, there are other incentives.

I have asked our sales representative, _____, to contact you in the next few days to answer any questions that may have come to mind since we last talked.

Sincerely,

3. LETTERS OF INVITATION TO ATTEND DEALER MEETING

If your company markets thru dealers, it probably holds periodic dealer meetings to announce new product lines, or to launch major advertising or sales promotion programs. Many sales organizations hold dealer training meetings. Since the dealer is an independent business man, getting his attendance at meetings such as these may be something of a problem. Of course, much depends on the reputation of your dealer meetings for providing benefits to the dealer that make it worthwhile for him to attend.

But beyond your reputation for good meetings, each meeting must be sold to the dealer organization. A letter is a good tool for introducing and selling such meetings.

Model Letter 14-5

Dear _____

With everybody shouting it, it must be true!!

19____ *is going to be the best year yet for the_____ industry.* The 19____ _____*(product name)*_____ product line is outstanding with many of the new features you have told us your customers want. Competition's eyes will bulge when they see what they're up against.

And we've been working for nine months to make sure the message gets across to your customers—a great advertising program with a new co-op program to help you get your advertising message across in your own area.

We've come up with an outstanding incentive program that will mean extra profits to you. Besides, we have a big suprise in store—a new incentive idea you're going to love.

But I can't spill all the beans now. Just make sure you come to the Dealer Annual Kick-Off Meeting. The attached sheet gives you all the lowdown. Don't miss it!

Sincerely,

Model Letter 14-6

Dear _____

One of the frustrations of being a dealer and running a sales force is trying to find good salesmen. We realize it's been a headache.

But it's interesting to observe that while most dealers have experienced the frustration, the problem is by no means universal. Some seem to have found the answer.

We'd like to help. So we've scheduled a symposium for January 14 at _____. Just 16 dealers have been invited, so the company will be select. To help us think through our mutual problem, we've asked _____, a well-respected authority on the subject of recruiting sales people, to be with us. He'll have some ideas to contribute, but, also, it'll be a time of discussion—a chance to talk about our salesman recruiting problems and what can be done about them.

Plan to attend this important one-day session. It could be the most profitable eight hours you've spent in a long time. Just check off and mail the enclosed post card. We'll do the rest.

Sincerely,

4. LETTER OF INVITATION TO AN OPEN HOUSE

The open-house is a perennial favorite traffic builder of businesses everywhere. And little wonder. Even its name speaks of friendly openness. Open-house events have been held for almost every imaginable occasion—new plant or office facilities, new management, a major change in product line, customer appreciation.

Whatever the reason for the open house, solid promotion of the event is the foundation of success. What better way to announce an open house than with a letter.

Model Letter 14-7

Dear _____

You're invited to an office-warming party. You see, we've

moved to our brand new, beautiful office facility here at
_____, but it will never seem like home till our
friends have crossed its threshhold.

So we've set aside Friday, April 5 as a special happening.
We'll have some refreshments and pretty girls to hand them
out. We plan to make some nice door prizes available just as
an added incentive (As if any were needed).

Merely return the enclosed postcard to let us know to expect
you. And then drop by any time from 1 to 6 p.m.

Sincerely,

Model Letter 14-8

Dear _____

Our new 50,000 sq. ft. warehouse is now ready to serve you—
and such service the hardware industry has never before seen.
With the latest in plant layout to facilitate rapid, same-day
delivery—with computerized order processing and filling—
with palletized truck loading—ours is a warehouse you just
must see to believe.

And that leads to the point of this letter. We would be most
pleased if you would drop by any time during the week of
June 6 for a guided tour of our new warehouse facility. We're
inviting you and some other of our friends and customers to
see just how their orders will be quickly and accurately
handled.

Just give us a ring a little in advance and plan to take about
an hour. You will be pleased with what we have done and we
will be pleased to have you visit us.

Sincerely,

Model Letter 14-9

Many of your neighbors have already responded. If you haven't, please mail your card today!

_____

_____ _____ _____ is inviting a
select group of your area's key executives to view the 19____
version of the _____ Traveling Trade Show.

Mr. Mike O'Hare, your sales representative for _____, will be in charge of this program which will feature _____'s newest techniques and ideas in the field of marking and labeling.

He will document his presentation with film, demonstrations and actual samples, drawing upon thousands of case histories in the marking and labeling field.

The showing will be held on Wednesday, April 23, at 1:30 p.m. and will last no more than an hour and a half.

Your early response to this invitation will be appreciated.

Cordially,

15

LETTERS THAT KEEP CUSTOMERS DURING A COMPANY CRISIS

15

LETTERS THAT KEEP
CUSTOMERS DURING
A COMPANY CRISIS

Every company makes errors. The simple fact that humans are involved insures the continuance of this truth. Deliveries are not made when promised. Customers are not provided the attention and care they deserve. The company fails to provide necessary personnel to service the customer's needs.

The temptation is to ignore such company shortcomings. Perhaps the customer won't notice the problem. Maybe we can get it corrected before it blows up in our face. Such a customer relations approach eventually will cause problems and lost customers.

A more appropriate response is to head off possible complaints by acknowledging problems and errors before the customer has the opportunity to complain. Not only is the customer more likely to forgive the error, but, if handled properly, such problems can be turned to something of an asset by helping the customer to realize that your company, too, is made up of striving humans.

1.   EXPLAINING DELIVERY DELAYS AND SELLING THE BENEFITS OF WAITING

Strikes, temporary inventory problems, shipping delays, unexpectedly high demand for a product and other circumstances beyond our control may occasionally make immediate delivery impossible. We want to do everything we can to convince our prospects and customers to wait for our product rather than buy from a competitor. The following letters aim at that result.

Model Letter 15-1

Dear _____

We're sorry to tell you that our warehouse employees at this **(a)** location will be on strike effective Monday, February 10, 19_____. We'll do our best to resolve the issues quickly. We're hopeful the strike will end shortly.

In the meantime, we have made preparations to supply your urgent requirements from this location with an emergency work crew of management personnel. We have also arranged alternate supply sources and have worked out a fast method of shipping your requirements from another regional warehouse.

We hope you'll bear with us during this period and excuse any delays. We will do everything we can to resolve the strike rapidly and to serve your needs in the meantime.

Many thanks for your cooperation.

Sincerely,

Alternate Wording:

(a)   We are sorry to inform you that our manufacturing plants will be on strike beginning February 10, 19_____.

We are doing our utmost to resolve the issues as quickly as possible. In the meantime, we believe we will be able to fill your orders as usual. We have made preparations for this possibility by stockpiling product for the past several months. In so long as the stock last, we will fill orders as usual.

Model Letter 15-2

Dear _____

For the last two weeks I have been trying to decide whether to cry or smile.

I want to thank you for the large order you just placed for our new line of _____. This line is definitely a "winner" and will be a fast moving, profitable item in your store. Unfortunately, you and many of our other customers were quicker and more accurate in assessing the full potential of this product in the marketplace than we were. Our initial production for this line wasn't high enough to completely fill all of the orders we received.

We have already begun increasing our production capacity. **(a)** For a short period, however, we have been forced to set up an allocation system to assure fair treatment of all of our customers.

We have shipped one-half of your order today under this system. We will ship one-fourth of your order in two weeks and the last one-fourth the week after that. By that time we expect to have the production capacity to fill all re-orders for the product immediately.

Thank you for your cooperation. I know this product will be a major contributor to your volume and profit this year. We are doing everything in our power to maximize your sales by filling your order as quickly as possible.

Sincerely,

Alternate Wording:

(a) We have already begun increasing our production capacity. For a short period, however, we will be forced to rely on a hot-line locator system for our dealers. The system is provided for legitimate sales only and works this way. Just call the toll-free number provided on the attached card and we will track down a unit close to you being held in stock by another dealer. All you have to do is pay freight from his point to yours. We'll handle credits and invoicing.

2. DELIVERY ERRORS

Perhaps the most frustrating thing that can happen to a sales manager is a foulup in delivery to an important customer or a new account the salesman has gone all out to sell. Fast action is called for. The emphasis must be on what is being done to satisfy the customer and reassurance that this won't happen again. The customer is more interested in action and a description of what is being done than an effort to place blame.

Model Letter 15-3

Dear _____

Everything arrived but the gasket kit! I had the requested **(a)** quantity of kits sent to you special delivery as soon as you phoned.

In the meantime we were able to dig into our packing and shipping system to determine why the error occured. As a result we have stiffened up the final inspection procedure to preclude this type of error from recurring.

I hope the kits reached you in time to prevent disruption of your production schedule. The new procedures we have installed will prevent this happening again.

Sincerely,

Alternate Wording:

(a) My most sincere apologies for shorting you on your recent order. Our sales representative will deliver the short item when he calls next Wednesday.

Model Letter 15-4

Dear _____

Haste does make waste!

As a result of our haste to insure fast delivery of your order, we attempted to deliver 12 tons of product to the lobby of your home office building. Believe me, we have learned the hard way that your home office is in Philadelphia and your manufacturing plant is in Pittsburgh.

The shipment was re-routed immediately and arrived at your plant approximately one-half day later than promised. My understanding of the situation is that your plant manager was worried for several hours, but that our mistake did not disrupt your production schedule.

We are paying the extra freight, of course. Frankly, we were guilty of trying too hard to impress you with the speed of our service. This was our first chance to serve you and the order was highest priority. Let me assure you that we won't stop trying—and we will take that extra minute to double check everything next time.

Sincerely,

3. PRODUCT RECALLS

This seems to be the age of product recalls, not only with automotive products of which we read so much in the news but in many other areas as well.

A letter announcing a potential hazard and indicating your company's intention for correcting it must be carefully worded to prevent conveying to the owner that the product is in any way inferior or that he must press the panic button until the product problem is corrected. This letter handles the problem very nicely.

Model Letter 15-5

Dear _____

We have learned that there is a slight chance of an electrical shock occuring to the operator of the _____ model steam table when certain unlikely conditions are present. The attachment describes the conditions which are necessary.

There is no need to discontinue using the unit unless conditions are present as described in the attachment.

Although the chances are slight, we are taking immediate steps to correct the situation. As representative will be calling at your plant within the next few days to add a ground wire to the unit.

We apologize for this inconvenience and promise that we will take the utmost of precautions to prevent it from happening again. The safety of your workers is too important to us to be taken lightly. As a result _____ equipment has been designed to be among the safest in the world.

Sincerely,

4. DISCONTINUING COMPLIMENTARY SERVICE

It is difficult to cut back services which customers have come to expect. But rising costs and shrinking profit margins sometimes force us to discontinue complimentary services our market has come to expect and take for granted.

Model Letter 15-6

Dear _____

We believe our customers appreciate our policy of offering quality merchandise at the lowest possible price. In these days of rising costs, some complimentary services which once could be provided must be discontinued.

With mixed feelings we are discontinuing our policy of free home delivery of any item purchased in our store. We will continue to offer home delivery service at a charge which only defrays our costs.

Sincerely,

Model Letter 15-7

Dear _____

Beginning the 1st of the month, we will offer our automatic inventory control service as an optional service at a small charge.

We have always taken pride in the service we provided our customers and no one else in the industry has provided an inventory control service. We also offer our customers prices as low or lower than anyone in the industry.

We intend to continue providing the highest quality product at a competitive price. We regret that rising costs will no longer allow us to provide inventory control service without charge. However, by offering the automatic inventory control service at the optional, small charge we believe we are providing the highest quality product and service at a low price.

Sincerely,

5. REPAIRING RELATIONS WITH CUSTOMERS WHO HAVE BEEN OFFENDED BY COMPANY REPRESENTATIVES

No matter how carefully a sales manager attempts to oversee communication with valued customers, occasionally a slip-up will occur and a customer will be offended. The following letter was sent to a customer who was mistakenly sent a strong collection letter.

Model Letter 15-8

Dear _____

I want to apologize for the letter mistakenly sent to you by our credit department. You have every right to be upset with us.

I offer you the choice of one of the following methods of reparation:

(Check One)

☐ Let me off the hook and accept my sincere apology.

☐ I will report to your office at 8:00 a.m. Monday and you may hit me in the face with a pie (this was suggested by your salesman, Tom _____. He offered to drive me over).

☐ Insist I fire the clerk in our credit department who sent out the letter. (His name is Bob Cratchit and he has a son named Tiny Tim. He is very sorry about the mistake.)

Seriously, when I allow an embarrassing mistake like this to happen, especially to as valued and prompt paying an account as you, it is unforgivable. It won't happen again.

Sincerely,

Unless the company has made the effort to train their service personnel to be customer relations and sales minded, they can occasionally irritate customers.

Model Letter 15-9

Dear _____

You're right! Bob _____ is outspoken, disrespectful, irascible and has the capacity to be downright obnoxious.

He is also the best mechanic I have ever known. That is why we sent him out to set up your machine when time was a factor. Bob is one of those men who seems to relate better to machinery than to people. We tolerate his idiosyncrasies in the shop here because his genius with machinery is invaluable and, frankly, I guess we've gotten used to his personality.

I apologize for the disruption I caused by sending him out. It **(a)** was my mistake and I won't include him on a service crew again.

Sincerely,

Alternate Wording:

(a)   While we intended to get your equipment operating quickly and efficiently, we certainly didn't plan to cause such disruptions to your personnel. We've decided the best way to get Bob's expertise while curbing his tongue is to team him with a more highly skilled diplomat. That will be our procedure in the future.

I apologize for the disruption I caused by sending him alone to your plant last week. It won't happen again.

6. WHEN AN ACCOUNT IS WITHOUT A SALES OR SERVICE REPRESENTATIVE

The unexpected loss of a salesman or a service representative can result in problems for your customers. If the customers are not assured that their needs will continue to be satisfied during the period they are without a sales or service representative, they will take their business elsewhere.

Model Letter 15-10

Dear _____

Please consider me as your sales representative for the next **(a)** thirty days.

As you know, Jack left us unexpectedly. We fully intend to continue providing you with a professional representative to serve your needs and are presently considering several qualified men.

In the meantime, you are stuck with me. Please phone me **(a)** (_____ direct line) when I can be of service. Two of our best salesmen _____ and _____ will be helping me serve your needs. The three of us will do our best for you.

I promise you that the care we are taking in selecting your new sales representative will make the short wait worthwhile.

Thanks for your cooperation.

Sincerely,

Alternate Wording:

(a) Please consider Bill Caldwell as your sales representative for the next thirty days.

(a) We have relieved Bill of some of his other responsibilities so he can provide you with the care you deserve. When you need his service you can contact him at _____. In the meantime you can expect him to make calls at your office with the same frequency as did Jack.

Model Letter 15-11

Dear _____

By the time you read this letter you will probably have heard about the automobile mechanics' strike. The dealers association will make every effort to resolve the situation quickly and fairly. In the meantime, my main concern is that you are able to obtain any service you may require on your 19____ _____.

I have attached a list of dealers outside of this area who will not be affected by the strike and also a list of local service stations and garages who have competent mechanics and adequate facilities to deal with normal maintenance. Please phone me personally at (_____ direct line) if you have an extraordinary service need and I will personally see that your needs are satisfied.

We expect this situation to be remedied in a short time.

I will personally do everything I can to assure that you will not be inconvenienced.

Thank you for working with us.

Sincerely,

Model Letter 15-12

Dear _____

Sam Wilkins has resigned from his position of service engineer and will be leaving us in two weeks.

We are assigning two neighboring service engineers, Curtis Johnson and Brian Engel, to service your equipment until a permanent replacement is assigned. We are assigning two men to assure that you will not have to wait for service. Please call Jim Bloss, the service manager, or me whenever you need a service engineer. Jim or I will see that you receive prompt service.

We hope to have a permanent service engineer assigned to you within thirty days. Thank you for your cooperation during this interim period. I promise you that the care we are taking in selecting your new service engineer will make the short wait worthwhile.

Sincerely,

16

LETTERS THAT TURN
LOST ACCOUNTS INTO
PRODUCING ACCOUNTS

16

LETTERS THAT TURN
LOST ACCOUNTS INTO
PRODUCING ACCOUNTS

How many times should you attempt to bring the lost account back into the buying fold? Many will tell you the proverbial seven times seventy.

What sales manager has been so fortunate as never to have lost a customer? Personalities clash, dissatisfactions occur, better opportunities seem present. Although customers stray, they also return. Conditions change and other companies make mistakes also. So perhaps it is a valid point that a lost customer should never be abandoned.

Certainly the personal sales call is the most forceful method for keeping close to the lost customer. But over a protracted period, repeated calls with no results may be prohibitively costly. So the letter also has value. Many managers program a continuous mail campaign to keep in touch with the lost account and to keep their company's name before the customer should a change in conditions occur.

To be successful, such a direct mail campaign with lost customers should:

- Be programmed on a regular basis. It's indeed fortunate when a single letter convinces the lost customer to renew his relationship. A personal letter every few months to keep your name before him and to tell him that you value his business is usually necessary.
- Be closely tailored to show correction of the problem that caused him to break the relationship. If you are aware of the reason you lost the customer, refer to correction of that ocndition in your letter. If you don't know why you lost him, you will want to use a more general approach. Or perhaps you can use a probing letter as is provided in Model Letter 16-3.

The letters which follow are provided in categories according to the appeal used to secure the customer's interest.

1. AN APPEAL ON THE BASIS OF PAST RELATIONSHIP

Even when a customer is no longer buying from your company, there may remain some feeling of relationship that can be relied on to reactivate a buying status. Perhaps the customer has just drifted away. Or perhaps a competitor has made an offer that temporarily seems more attractive. As long as his reason is not great, a simple "we've missed you" letter may get him on the buying list again. Such is the following letter.

Model Letter 16-1

Dear _____

We Miss You!

Yes, every one of our customers is important to us. And we take special note when they haven't bought from us for a time.

It's been several months since you made a purchase from (a) _____. Maybe the reason has been small. Or big. But won't you come back. We miss you!

Sincerely,

Alternate Wording:

(a) You have not purchased from us in several months. Whatever the reason, we want to do whatever is necessary to earn your business. We miss you!

If yours is a retail business that uses its own charge account system, you will be able to locate inactive customers from idle charge accounts. This letter can tell these inactives you miss them.

Model Letter 16-2

Dear _____

You haven't used your _____ charge account for some time. That means you may be missing some tremendous values.

You will always find special values at _____. And your charge account is an especially convenient way to take advantage of them.

Stop in soon, won't you? Our charge account customers are especially valued. And we'll show it.

Sincerely,

When the customer strays, the reason may be unknown to you or the salesman. This letter probes for the reason. It makes a light, easy to read method for learning the nature of a problem.

Model Letter 16-3

Dear _____

It's been some time since you've bought from us and that grieves us terribly. If we goofed, please give us a chance to correct it.

Just check off "Why" and return this letter in the enclosed addressed envelope. Maybe we can help out.

☐ We haven't needed to replenish inventory, lately. We'll be ordering again sometime soon.

☐   Have your salesman call. We'd like to place an order.

☐   Yes, you goofed. But tell your salesman to call. Maybe we can work it out.

Thanks! We appreciate your candid comments.

Sincerely,

2. AN APPEAL BASED ON A CHANGE IN PERSONNEL

The appeal to the inactive customer to buy once again from your company is most likely to be effective when closely related to the cause of the separation. For those customers who drifted away because of friction with some member of your organization these letters are valuable.

Model Letter 16-4

Dear _____

We've put on a new service face—new service manager— **(a)** New service organization. All to serve you better.

It's been some time since you bought from us. Won't you give us a try. You'll be pleased with the changes you find.

Sincerely,

Alternate Wording:

(a)   We have a brand new organization ready to serve you. Your new sales representative will be calling on you soon to see how we can meet your needs. Our new service manager has built a capable service team to serve you better than ever before.

Model Letter 16-5

Dear _____

An old wive's tale says "The new broom sweeps clean." And we intend to prove it's so.

Hello! I've just been appointed sales manager for _____. We plan to prove ourselves to you by making the changes in our organization you've been asking for. We think you'll be pleased with our new face.

_____, your sales representative, tells me it has been some time since you have placed an order with us. He also tells me he is firmly convinced that some of the changes we have recently made will open the door to a new relationship between us. He plans to call you this week for an appointment to explain our new policies and programs to you.

In addition, I will be calling you for an appointment to meet you personally.

Sincerely,

3.   AN APPEAL BASED ON REVISED POLICIES

When old policies have prevented a customer from continuing a buying relationship with you, this letter may serve to reactivate him.

Model Letter 16-6

Dear _____

We've made a change in our organization and we think you'll like it.

The size of our sales representative territories has been **(a)** reduced to permit more frequent calls on our customers and more individualized attention to your needs. You can expect a call from the _____ Representative on alternate weeks now. As a result you can expect fewer special orders and less time between deliveries.

_____, will be calling on you Tuesday, March 5 and on alternate Tuesday's thereafter. He will be happy to help you inventory your stock and prepare an order.

Sincerely,

Alternate Wording:

(a)   We have introduced a new credit policy which includes cash discounts and other favorable terms which we believe will be interesting to you. We also now offer an inventory service which could reduce your present investment in stock.

4.   AN APPEAL BASED ON A NEW PRODUCT

Occasionally you may be unable to satisfy a customer's unusual needs from your standard line. When a product later becomes available which will meet his specifications, you will want to advise him and solicit his business. Although the salesman will have the primary responsibility for notifying the customer of the new product, a letter from you will assist the salesman to prepare the customer.

Model Letter 16-7

Dear _____

Last year you provided us with a challenge we were unable to meet. We were unable to provide you with the particular type sprayer nozzle to handle your oil coating application. That doesn't often happen.

As we talked with other companies with similar manufacturing applications, we became aware of a new marketing opportunity.

Our engineering department loves challenges, and did they ever respond to the one you provided them. We think our new Model 620B sprayer nozzle will meet precisely the needs you described to us earlier.

Our Sales Representative, _____, will be calling you this week for an appointment to describe and demonstrate this new product.

Sincerely,

5. AN APPEAL BASED ON A SPECIAL SALE

Perhaps only inertia is keeping the customer from initiating a purchase. Many products are bought on a discretionary basis. The customer may buy or delay depending on his sense of priorities at the moment. Getting him to buy requires a special reason to act now. Here is a letter that is designed to jolt the infrequent buyer into action.

Model Letter 16-8

Dear _____

Would you believe that 24 months have passed since you bought your ___*(model car)*___ from us? It's about now that many of our customers begin to think about a new model. We'd like to encourage you to come in to see the 19____ **(a)** model _____. To do that I've enclosed a coupon worth a free lubrication and oil change on me. And while your car is in for servicing, I'll give your car an appraisal for trade in on a 19____. While you're waiting maybe you would like to take a look at and test drive a beautiful *(model)*

Just call me and I'll set up an appointment with our service **(b)** people. That way you can be sure of taking only a minimum time to get your car serviced.

Sincerely,

Alternate Wording:

(a) We'd like you to experience many new features, increased gas mileage, and responsiveness of the 19____. To accomplish that I would like to lend you my own new _____ for a full day next Saturday. When you pick up my car I'll give your car an appraisal for trade in on a 19____. Used car prices have been increasing and you may be pleasantly surprised.

(b) I'll phone you Wednesday to confirm this arrangement. I know you'll enjoy driving the 19____ _____ as much as I do.

6. AN APPEAL BASED ON NEW EXPERTISE

Some products and many services are sold only with considerable backup experience. This experience is an added feature that accompanies the sale to make the product of greater value to the customer. The sale of some products and services is so heavily dependent on such backup expertise that a sale is difficult without it. When new experience is acquired, new sales opportunities are opened up. Here is a model letter that was written on such an occasion. Although not a dead account, this situation represents business that may be newly available.

Model Letter 16-9

Dear _____

We have been providing many of your banking services for some time and we're mighty proud of it.

However, we have not yet been able to convince you to use our payroll processing program. That may be understandable when you consider that at the time we last talked to you about it, we had no direct experience in your unique industry or union situation.

But now we have considerable experience—not only in the same industry in which you are involved, but with the same union. In fact, we believe our experience with other similar companies will be invaluable to you as you consider our payroll processing system for your own company.

Like to hear more about how our payroll system has worked for these other companies—how it has saved them money and time and has provided them with the reports they require when they need them?

I'll call you next Monday for an appointment.

Sincerely,

17

LETTERS THAT PUT CUSTOMERS AND INFLUENTIAL THIRD PARTIES ON YOUR SALES TEAM

LETTERS THAT PUT
CUSTOMERS AND
INFLUENTIAL THIRD PARTIES
ON YOUR SALES TEAM

The letters in this chapter aim to produce tangible, right-now results in the form of additional sales to new prospects, support of outside influences who can sway a sale, and increased commitment to your company and product by present customers.

Your present satisfied customers may be one of your most valuable assets for producing additional sales. Their testimony in your behalf to prospects can have a great influence on the buyer's decision. There may be influential experts in your market whose opinion of your product can sway the purchaser. If your product is a "big ticket item" which is usually purchased with outside financing, the banker or finance source's opinion of your product may influence the outcome of the sale. If you sell a consumer item, promotional activities featuring satisfied customers can bring you and your product favorable publicity and additional sales. And if you are selling to a broad market of consumers, the current consumer movement can provide a challenge to your marketing intelligence and imagination, resulting in greater customer satisfaction and loyalty to your quality product rather than a "bogey man" to be feared.

1. REQUESTING CUSTOMER TESTIMONIALS

Testimonials or referrals from satisfied customers can be powerful sales tools. We can be more certain of their cooperation if we explain exactly what help we are requesting from the customer, make it easy for him to comply, and thank him for his help in specific ways. One caution in thanking these customers for their help: sales managers who have been successful in securing customer testimonials agree that small and thoughtful "thank you's" are most appropriate and insure future cooperation. A thank-you letter or phone call, occasional friendly lunch or invitation to a ball game are appropriate—but large gifts appear to be bribes and can insult the integrity of the satisfied customer.

Model Letter 17-1

Dear _____

I'm asking a small favor which will take you only a few **(a)** minutes.

You have been a valued customer of ours for several years and have re-ordered many times and expressed satisfaction with our products and service.

If I'm not taking too much for granted, would you be willing **(b)** to drop me a note telling me just what your experience with our product and service has been; what kind of a job we have done for you, and where we have been able to help you save time and money in your operation? Your experiences would be most helpful to me in presenting our product to buyers in other industries (not competitors of your company).

A pre-addressed, stamped envelope is enclosed, and if it would be more convenient, just use the back of this sheet for your letter.

Many thanks.

Sincerely,

Alternate Wording:

(a) Would you be interested in telling others what ___*(product name)*___ has meant to you?

(b) If I'm not taking too much for granted, would you be willing to drop me a note telling me in what ways our product has been most helpful to you. Your opinion concerning ways our product has helped you cut costs and increase productivity would be appreciated.

Model Letter 17 2

Dear _____

I enjoyed visiting with you the other day. I am happy to know that you have been pleased by the service we provide.

May I have your permission to refer to you and your company when discussing our product with other companies? As you know, many buyers are interested in the experiences of others when they are purchasing from a supplier for the first time. Your company's high standards are well known and respected.

Rest assured that we will provide the same satisfaction to these new accounts that we have provided you.

Sincerely,

The sales manager who provided the following letter represents a product which is difficult to demonstrate and visualize except in existing installations. He is requesting visitation privileges, to actually "tour" prospects to a satisfied customer's facility. This can be an effective sales tool even with products which can be visualized and demonstrated in simpler ways.

Model Letter 17-3

Dear _____

I've been thinking about your company ever since my visit last week and have decided to ask you for a favor.

You know how difficult our product is to describe to **(a)** someone who is not already using it. However, when a prospect observes it in use, he can't help but be impressed wtih the obvious quality, efficiency and economy. Well, I would like to use your operation as an example with a company currently considering us. Would you allow me to bring them over to tour your facility? I want to do this at a time most convenient to you and will be careful not to disrupt your operation in any way. I would appreciate it if you would personally act as our guide. I will also be sure t absent myself for a few minutes during the tour to insure that my prospective sutomers feel free to discuss our product with you in private.

I will phone you later this week to discuss this proposed tour. I'm proud you and your company are customers and believe our product speaks for itself when observed in your operation.

If this project will fit into your schedule without inconveniencing you, I'll certainly appreciate it.

Sincerely,

Alternate Wording:

(a) As you know, one of the most important benefits our customers receive by using our product is the ease and efficiency with which it is integrated with allied equipment. ut unfortunately that's a benefit that must be seen to be appreciated.

This letter is sent after a tour to thank the customer for fisitation privileges. Notice that in this case the writer was able to point out specific benefits the customer had received by allowing the sales manager to tour the facility.

Model Letter 17-4

Dear _____

My thanks again for allowing me to tour your facility last Tuesday with a group of potential customers. They were enthusiastic about our product as a result of the tour and two orders have already been placed.

They were also impressed with the efficiency of your entire (a) operation and with your attention to quality control. As you mentioned to me on Tuesday, several of them did represent companies who should be prospects for your product. I'll be glad to pass along this information to your salesmen.

Thanks again for your hospitality and cooperation.

I'd like to come over next week and discuss the possibility of doing this again sometime in the future if you agree this project was advantageous to both of our companies.

Sincerely,

Alternate Wording:

(a) They were also impressed with your modern operation and particularly with the efficiency with which the plant is laid out. You must be very proud of what you have been able to accomplish and deservedly so.

Please accept my personal thanks and also the thanks of those who visited your plant. You have benefited not only me, but those who may be able to utilize our equipment as you have.

2. SEEKING OUTSIDE FINANCING

If you are selling capital equipment or a big ticket item of any type, the more sources of financing you can depend upon to finance your customer, the better. Many sales organizations selling products requiring financing devote much attention to "selling" finance sources such as banks, insurance companies, and commercial finance companies. They do this so that their qualified customers will have ready access to funds and a choice of terms and also to insure that the lender will see their product as a good investment and an attractive loan. The writer of this letter uses it with success to open communication with banks and insurance companies.

Model Letter 17-5

Dear _____

Many sound, aggressive lenders are seeking substantial investment opportunities in the agricultural community. As a supplier to agriculture, we are looking to establish a working relationship with such a company.

Outstanding management, profit projections, cash flows, es- **(a)** tate planning, market knowledge, adequate collateral, and nutritional expertise are what we look for in an agribusiness man with whom we work. Marketing _____, _____ and _____ equipment as we do often requires the implementation of a totally new meat or milk plant such as buildings, feed handling equipment, milking parlors, large expanses of concrete and in some cases the land itself. These packages range from $50,000 to $600,000, normally requiring long-term real estate financing.

May we have the privilege of visiting with you or your key agricultural loan staff member to explore methods by which we can lead you to sound investments and assist your agribusiness customer in finding long-term financial assistance.

Please contact me at your earliest convenience if you would like to explore this opportunity.

Sincerely,

Alternate Wording:

(a) We market a product that produces a rapid payout for the user. Depreciation is minimal and the resale market is sound. In short, it provides an excellent investment opportunity for agriculturally oriented financial institutions.

3. PROMOTIONAL ACTIVITIES FEATURING CUSTOMERS

Particularly if you sell a consumer item, you have the opportunity to feature customers in your promotional activities. The following letter emphasizes a product value and, in addition, is a good public relations effort with a popular appeal to the local news media as a humorous human interest story. Although this classic promotional activity was submitted by a successful marketer of a consumer good, with a little imagination the general concept might be used even with heavy industrial goods if an interesting and newsworthy presentation to a customer is included.

Model Letter 17-6

Dear _____

Congratulations for helping to prove there's always room for one more in a Volkswagen. We would like to present you and your husband with a savings bond which we hope will be used toward your son's education.

Since 19___, when we started the Bonds-for-Babies program, we have awarded savings bonds to 302 children. We are making arrangements with your dealer and area distributor to present this bond to you. I am sure you will be hearing from them shortly.

Meanwhile, I hope you will enjoy driving your Volkswagen for a long time to come—even if you never again have a trip as eventful as the one of May 10!

Sincerely,

4. RESPONDING TO CONSUMER QUESTIONS

If you are selling to a broad market of consumers, you may occasionally receive inquiries or questions from concerned consumers or consumer activist groups. These inquiries are not to be handled lightly, and your company may have a policy and procedure for responding to them (see Chapter 18).

The following letter is included only to show that such inquiries can be opportunities for positive communication and can result in more understanding of the value of the product or service and greater customer satisfaction.

Model Letter 17-7

Dear _____

Thanks for stating your concerns about Ohio Bell's advertising and *Hello*. These questions certainly are warranted, and I welcome the opportunity to explain why we use such communication tools to reach you and other customers with information about how to make the best use of your telephone service.

First, to your specific question—the cost of *Hello*. Each *Hello* is produced for about 1/2¢ per customer and it rides along postage-free in the bill envelope. Every month it reaches about 2 1/3 million customers who rate it above television, radio and newspapers in providing them useful information about their service.

Your suggestion that the elimination of *Hello* and advertising would cut expenses and benefit customers is understandable. Unfortunately, such an expense reduction would increase your telephone bill—not decrease it. Ohio Bell spends this money to communicate with customers for three reasons: 1. to improve employee and equipment efficiency by telling customers how to use the telephone properly; 2. to increase revenue through sales such as long distance and extensions; 3. to help customers get more value out of their service. Here are some examples of how advertising and *Hello* benefit you and Ohio Bell.

- We encourage you to use your directory rather than call an information operator to locate numbers—that holds down people and equipment costs.

- We suggest that customers dial long distance calls themselves rather than using an operator—that saves you money and cuts expenses at the same time. A recent Bell System study shows that $100 is saved in operating costs for every $1 spent to advertise customer dialing of long distance calls.

- We pass along dozens of tips about the proper use of your telephone especially through *Hello*—customers follow this information ad get more value from their telephone.

- We advertise to sell more optional telephone services like extensions, Trimline and Princess which increase revenue. Revenue produced in this manner decreases the amount that we have to ask to offset the effects of inflation.

Despite this evidence, you may continue to feel there is something wrong about the telephone company spending money to advertise. You can be sure we will continue explaining why this benefits both the company and its customers. I prefer to respond to this concern rather than the one which you and all customers and shareholders would raise if we were to discontinue use of these communication tools. Then we could be accused of irresponsible management action for ignoring opportunities to save money. Against that charge, I would have no defense.

I hope this answers your questions. If you would like to discuss it, please let me know.

Sincerely,

18

WHEN NOT TO WRITE LETTERS

18

WHEN NOT TO WRITE
LETTERS

Even in this age of electronic communication wonders, it is difficult to imagine conducting business without the benefit of letters. Their value in conveying ideas is without challenge. Yet, on occasion, a letter may not be the most appropriate means to express your idea. We have mentioned several such instances in previous chapters. This chapter is devoted completely to such considerations.

1. WHEN PERSONAL CONTACT IS MORE EFFECTIVE

Face-to-face or telephone communication possesses certain strengths over the written word. For example, consider these occasions when the spoken word may be more effective:

- *When confidentiality is important.* Certain messages are for the receive only. Should others read your letter, embarrassment, competitive advantage or other problems might occur.

251

For example, severe salesman discipline problems should be handled personally. One important reason for this personal touch is that no one should know of the discipline action other than you and the salesman.

Confidentiality is generally also important where newly developed products are involved. Many companies restrict their use of letters concerning new products or marketing ideas until they are sufficiently well developed to assure that competition will not be able to secure a competitive edge with the product or idea.

Of course, one solution to the public quality of the letter is to mark it "personal and confidential," which is still done in many companies. This technique seems to work reasonably well at least to keep the letter from being read by anyone other than the intended reader until he has the opportunity. The problem occurs when such letters are not handled with sufficient care at the receiving or sending end and prying eyes learn of their content after the receiver.

Generally, though, the best solution is to refrain from any letter that you wouldn't want prying eyes to read.

- *When body and facial responses are an important part of the message to be transmitted.* Some time ago the term "Body Language" was made popular as the means of determining what others are thinking by reading their body stances. We have all learned that certain facial expressions have special meaning to us. There is little doubt that we stand to learn more of the delicate meaning of the speaker and he of ours when personal, face-to-face talk is involved. Although such finely-tuned communication is not always required, when it is we should opt for the personal style that provides it.

  For example, discussing a salesman's drinking problem may require face-to-face contact not only for the personal nature of the problem, but to provide you with the opportunity to read the subtle body expressions he might provide. His glance to the floor when he makes his promise to stay off the bottle will tell you more than all his words.

- *To emphasize the importance of the message.* Whenever you wish to convey urgency or great importance, the spoken word, particularly face-to-face, is generally most effective. Making a special trip across town or to the next state has a way of conveying the message that whatever it is the speaker has to say must be of great importance. The salesman who knows his boss is making a special trip to talk with him is alerted to the meeting's importance. The customer who receives a personal call from the sales manager of his supplier knows the manager feels the call is important and, in addition, senses the importance with which the manager holds the customer.

2. WHEN IT'S IMPORTANT NOT TO COMMIT THE COMPANY

Letters can have a way of becoming official doctrine or law. This is especially true where union or activist groups are concerned. If you don't mean to commit the company to a particular point of view and you are writing to someone who intentionally or otherwise might misconstrue the meaning of your letter, best use the spoken word. Here are some examples:

- *Use the spoken word when a letter might be construed as a contract.* When you are dealing with salesmen or customers in sensitive areas and when you are not completely sure of your ground, it is better not to communicate in writing. For instance, in a dispute over commissions or terms of employment with a salesman, written communication should be avoided unless you are willing to have the terms provided in the letter bind the company as a legal contract.

  Today we are seeing more and more salesman unions. If you deal with a union, you have probably already found that you must always be sensitive to what you commit to writing unless you fully intend to obligate the company.

  The same can be true with customers. Pricing is often a delicate area especially where prices must be negotiated with the customer. Again written comments to the customer concerning price should not be made unless you intend to bind the company with your statement.

- *Resist writing letters when social action groups are attempting to trap or entice the company.* "Corporate gadfly" was once the term. "Consumer activist" is the popular label used today for the groups and individuals who question and criticize the way businesses are run.

  What response should a sales manager make to inquiries or criticisms from consumer or social action groups? In many instances, the answer is no response and particularly no written response. A small and seemingly insignificant comment made to an activist group can mushroom into a newsworthy item which can do great harm to your company's image and your sales.

When a written reply is made to such a group, it should be with the counsel of your legal department. They can assist you with the precise wording of your letter and can save the company much anguish.

You may be well advised to never reply to an individual concerning a social or activist issue and only to those groups which have established some reputation in the community. Some groups are formed on a shoestring, exist for a short while to harrass a few companies, and disolve again with little accomplished other than to leave the public with considerable false impressions. If you have not heard of the group, don't reply either orally or in writing until you have determined its legitimacy through the local newspaper or government agency.

Good advice is to consign such correspondence to a specialized department within your company. Special training is often required and when used can frequently turn a company problem into an asset. The letter included in Chapter 17, page 234 is an example.

3. WHEN TIMELINESS IS ESSENTIAL

Two, three day and up to one week delivery by the postal service is a common expectancy today. Slow mail deliveries can seriously hamper any communication dependent on timely expression of your thoughts to your reader. If speed is important, better use a telephone.

- *Use a telephone when customer satisfaction requires rapid handling.* When a customer problem occurs, speed is important. Take two or three days required for a letter and the customer will perceive the delay as a lack of interest on your part. If you should require any additional information from the customer, the handling of a customer complaint can run into weeks. That's a good lesson in how to lose a valuable customer.

The personal touch is most valuable when customer complaints are involved. Not only what the customer says, but how he says it can be determined more readily. And frequently the time required to work out the problem is reduced to minutes rather than days.

If a direct, personal meeting is impractical due to the distance involved, the telephone provides the next best method for resolving customer complaints. Although the telephone deprives us of some of the benefits of a face-to-face talk, it does convey the importance we place on the handling of the matter and does speed up the handling.

Whether handling the customer's problem involves a face-to-face talk or telephone, a letter can provide effective follow-up as described in Chapter 11.

- *The letter is not best for daily direction of salesmen.* The essence of the sales manager's job, to make the salesmen the best they can be, is best accomplished with face-to-face or telephone conversation. Daily direction requires close timing and quick feedback. Send a letter to direct a salesman to make a timely call on a prospect and competition may already have secured the account by the time the salesman receives the letter.

Day-to-day coaching is difficult to accomplish by letter. Coaching requires personal observation of how the salesman is performing. It requires the personal give and take to arrive at an awareness of key problems and the most effective solution.

All of the points made in this chapter on when not to write letters, of course, are just common sense. Perhaps the most important common sense rule is one that if followed would make all of the other ones unneeded. The general rule is to match the communication tool to the job to be accomplished. Just keep in mind that the letter allows less room for misinterpretation, but is less personal and less timely. The telephone or personal call can provide a greater sense of urgency and importance.